◀ TIMES LEARN

SPI
MALAY!

GW01033072

By the same author

Write Malay

◀ TIMES LEARN MALAY ▶

SPEAK MALAY!

Edward S King

B.A. (Hons.)

formerly Senior Lecturer in Linguistic Research,
Language Institute, Pantai Valley

A course in simple Malay for English-speaking Malaysians

The book of the radio programme
"Speak Malay!"
broadcast by Radio Malaya

TIMES BOOKS INTERNATIONAL
Singapore • Kuala Lumpur

New Edition 1988
Reprinted 1990, 1991, 1992, 1993, 1995

© **1986 TIMES EDITIONS PTE. LTD.**

Published by Times Books International
an imprint of Times Editions Pte. Ltd.

Times Centre, 1 New Industrial Road
Singapore 1953.

Times Subang
Lot 46, Subang Hi-Tech Industrial Park
Batu Tiga, 40000 Shah Alam
Selangor Darul Ehsan, Malaysia.

Printed by JBW Printers & Binders Pte. Ltd.

ISBN 981 204 129 X

PREFACE TO THE NEW EDITION

It is pleasing, and somewhat humbling, to know that after more than twenty-five years my little book has proved useful enough and popular enough to warrant yet another edition, for the preparation of which I am grateful to Times Books International.

My thanks are above all due to the people of Malaysia, who welcomed me and my family among themselves and who inspired me with a great love for their beautiful country and for the Malay language.

I hope that this small work will go some way towards inspiring that love in others and that at least some readers of 'Speak Malay!' will feel encouraged to continue their studies by making use of the sequel, 'Write Malay'. The two books really form a single complete course.

E.S. KING
August 1988

PREFACE

This book has grown out of a series of programmes entitled "Speak Malay!" which I wrote for Radio Malaya, and therefore shares both in the purpose and in the limitations of the Radio Course. The idea behind both the Radio Course and the present text-book is not only to provide the complete beginner with a properly graded course in simple spoken Malay, but also to help those English-speaking Asians who already know a little bazaar Malay to improve and increase their knowledge and bring it more into line with a standard acceptable to Malay ears. Both courses are designed to help students to avoid the worst errors of bazaar Malay, a lingua franca which most foreigners speak in the innocent belief that they are speaking real colloquial Malay. For convenience of reference I have grouped together some of the worst fallacies of bazaar Malay in Appendix D.

The present volume, like the Radio Course, makes no pretence at completeness. The scope of the Radio Course was severely limited by the amount of time available—five minutes a day for three months. It is clearly impossible to introduce a great deal of new material in the space of a five-minute broadcast, nor, indeed, is it desirable. It was therefore decided to concentrate on teaching a small but useful vocabulary together with the more important structures and patterns of spoken Malay, thereby providing the student with a solid basis on which to build for himself. I firmly believe that one of the main reasons for much of the bad Malay spoken in Malaya today is that in the past teachers have laid too much stress on vocabulary and not enough on structure, that is, too many words and not enough sentences.

This course is based entirely on the sentence, and it is therefore the sentences (Section A) of each lesson which are the most important part of the course. An intelligent student who studies the sentences carefully should be able to deduce the grammar for himself. The method used is that of "unconscious assimilation": that is to say that the student assimilates the language without realising it by means of the constant repetition of dozens of sentences all following the same pattern. Every new word is first introduced in a sentence or, more often, in several sentences. The word lists (Section B in each lesson) are given merely for the convenience of the student who wants to take stock of the new material he has learnt. The grammar sections (Section C in each lesson) are rather a commentary on the sentences than a systematic grammar of the language. The sentences are all-important and each set should be mastered before the student proceeds to the next lesson. This does not mean that they should be learnt by heart, but rather that they should be so thoroughly understood that it is no effort to rattle off others like them.

The course is arranged into weeks, each of five lessons; in addition, at the end of each week comes a revision lesson with translation and other exercises intended partly to give further practice in what has been studied during the week and partly to test the new-found knowledge. A key to these exercises has been provided towards the end of the volume.

Generally speaking, new structures are introduced on Mondays and Wednesdays, Tuesday and Thursday being used for practice in these new patterns and for the introduction of new vocabulary; Friday serves as a revision for the week's work. Here and there it has been found necessary to depart from this plan, for example in the teaching of the numerals and the way to tell the time.

To round off the book a number of appendices has been provided, each one dealing with some topic or other which for one reason or another was not dealt with in the body of the course. Finally all the words in the course (about 650) together with all those in the appendices, bringing the total to nearer a thousand words, have been arranged into a Malay-English and an English-Malay vocabulary at the end of the book.

My thanks are due to Radio Malaya, and in particular to Zainal Alam for his unstinting help and guidance in the preparation of the original radio series and to Felix Puerto for so gallantly fulfilling the role of guinea-pig in the experiment; to Tony Beamish for his advice and encouragement; and also to the staff of the Radio Malaya Station in Penang, who put in many long hours in the recording studio; to Hodder & Stoughton Educational for being interested enough to publish the volume; and last, but by no means least, to my wife for her constant encouragement and support throughout the venture — without her it is doubtful whether anything would have come of it.

If this book helps to awaken the interest of but a single student in the Malay language, and if it helps even a little in the wider spreading of the Bahasa Kebangsaan among Malayans, then my work will not have been in vain.

Kuala Lumpur   E.S.K.

CONTENTS

ABBREVIATIONS USED

adj.	*adjective*
adv.	*adverb*
cf.	*(Latin)* confer: *compare*
cl.	*classifier*
intrans.	*intransitive*
lit.	*literally*
n.	*noun*
rel.	*relative*
q.v.	*(Latin)* quod vide: *which see*
trans.	*transitive*
vb.	*verb*
viz	*(Latin)* videlicet: *that is to say*

THE PRONUNCIATION OF MALAY

The following notes make no pretence at being a dissertation on Malay phonetics. They are merely intended to help the student to avoid the worst faults made by non-Malay speakers when speaking the language, and to provide him with a pronunciation which, though not perfect, will be understood.

No written description of the phonetics of a language can ever take the place of the guidance of a native speaker. Imitate as closely as you can the way in which your Malay friends talk, even going as far as to copy their mannerisms and gestures. They will not be offended: on the contrary, the more you speak as they do, the more delighted they will be.

In pronunciation, perhaps even more than in grammar, idiom and vocabulary, Malay varies greatly from place to place. The following description is an attempt at a standard which will be acceptable anywhere, but once again you are advised to suit your Malay to the district in which you live. If your Malay friends pronounce differently from the way given here, then forget the book and imitate your friends.

Vowels

(1) A   This letter stands for the sound of *a* in *father,* although not so deep or long as the English sound; it is similar to the *u* in *but* (southern English) or almost identical with *a* in *man* as pronounced by a Yorkshireman. Examples:

makan   *eat*
pasar   *market*

At the end of a word, A is like the *a* in *China:*

| ada | *to be* |
| lada | *pepper* |

(2) E   This letter stands for the sound of *e* in *garden* or of *e* in *butter*. Examples:

besar	*big*
sedap	*tasty*
segan	*bashful*

(3) É   This letter stands for the sound of *e* in *bed* or, in some parts of the country for the *é* of French *été*. Examples:

méja	*table*
léwat	*late*
téngok	*look*

(4) I   This letter stands for the sound of *i* in *machine* or *ee* in *feet*. The sound is, however, shorter than the English sound. Examples:

manis	*sweet*
minum	*drink*
biji	*seed*

(5) O   This letter stands for a sound between the *aw* of *law* and the *oo* of *book*. It is not so open as the *o* of *pot* and does not taper off into a diphthong as does the *o* of southern English *hope* (ho-oop). The *o* of *hope* as pronounced in the north of England, however, comes very close to the Malay sound. Examples:

kosong	*empty*
tolong	*help*
kotor	*dirty*

(6) U   This letter stands for the sound of *oo* in *pool*, but it is a little shorter than the English sound. Examples:

lulus	*pass*
tujuh	*seven*
minum	*drink*

Diphthongs

Malay has only two diphthongs—AI and AU:

(7) AI   This combination is pronounced like the *ai* in English *aisle* or the *i* in *fine*, except that it is shorter. Examples:

sungai	*river*
tangkai	*stem*
bidai	*window blind*

(8) AU   This combination is pronounced like the *ow* of *how*. Examples:

pulau	*island*
daun	*leaf*
gaun	*dress*

Consonants

(9) B   As in English; but pronounced as *p* at the end of the word. Examples:

bapa	*father*
besar	*big*
menjawab	*answer* (*pron.* menjawap)

(10) C   English *ch* in *church* will do, but more accurately this sound is nearer the front of the mouth than the English *ch*. It is somewhere between *ch* of *church* and *t* of *tube*. Examples:

cari	*seek*
cawan	*cup*
kecil	*small*

(11) D   As in English; but pronounced as *t* at the end of a word. Examples:

hari Ahad	*Sunday (pron.* hari ahat*)*
Samad	*a man's name (pron.* Samat*)*
ada	*have*

(12) F   This letter stands for the English sound. The Malays, however, have great difficulty in pronouncing it as it is used only in foreign words and does not occur in pure Malay words. It is usually substituted by *p*. Examples:

| fasal | *reason (usually:* pasal*)* |
| Yusuf | *man's name (often:* Yusup*)* |

(13) G   Always as in *go;* never as in *gem*. Examples:

pergi	*go*
guru	*teacher*
pagar	*fence*

(14) GH   This combination, again, stands for an Arabic sound. It is the voiced counterpart of *kh* (q.v.) and sounds rather like the French throat-r. The Malays, however, often have difficulty in pronouncing it themselves, and frequently substitute a simple *g*. The student may safely follow their example. There are no words in this course involving this sound, and so you can safely forget about it for the time being at least.

(15) H   This represents the same sound as the English *h*. There are, however, some differences in application:

         (a) At the beginning of a word *h* in most cases may be safely dropped in pronunciation;

many Malay dialects do this:

hari	*day (or:* ari*)*
hujan	*rain (or:* ujan*)*
hutan	*jungle (or:* utan*)*

(b) In the middle of a word between two identical vowels, *h* is always clearly pronounced:

| léhér | *neck* |
| tahan | *support* |

(c) In the middle of a word between two dissimilar vowels, *h* is often elided in pronunciation:

tahu	*know (or:* tau*)*
tahun	*year (or:* taun*)*
pahit	*bitter (or:* pait*)*

(d) At the end of a word *h* must always be pronounced quite clearly and on no account omitted. This is quite difficult for English speakers, who need to practise this carefully:

belah	*to cut*
marah	*angry*
tujuh	*seven*

(16) J English *j* in *judge* will do, but more accurately this sound is nearer the front of the mouth than the English *j*. It is somewhere between the *j* of *judge* and the *d* of *duty*. Examples:

juta	*million*
tujuh	*seven*
jari	*finger*

(17) K Like the English *k* but without the puff of breath that usually accompanies the English *k*.

In English the Malay sound occurs after *s:* compare *cot* (kot) with *Scot* (skot). Examples:

kota	*fort*
kampung	*village*
kenduri	*feast*

For *k* at the end of a word, see the note below on the Glottal Catch.

(18) KH   This combination represents the sound of the Scots *ch* in *loch* or the German *ch* in *Achtung*. It is found only in Arabic loan-words and is often substituted by simple *k*. Examples:

khabar	*news (or:* kabar)
hari Khamis	*Thursday (or:* hari Kamis)

(19) L   This is more or less like the English *l*. The "dark" *l* of *ball*, *couple*, etc. does occur in some dialects but is better avoided by the student. The clear *l* of *leaf* should be used in all cases. Examples:

kapal	*ship*
tinggal	*stay*
léhér	*neck*

(20) M   Just like English *m*. Examples:

minum	*drink*
masam	*sour*
manis	*sweet*

(21) N   Like English *n*. Examples:

nasi	*cooked rice*
ini	*this*
kenduri	*feast*

(22) NY This combination stands for a sound similar to *ni* in *onion* or *n* in *news*. It is exactly like *gn* in French *montagne* or Spanish *ñ* in *señor*. Examples:

harganya	*the price*
nyamuk	*mosquito*
banyak	*a lot*

(23) NG This combination stands for the sound of *ng* in *sing* or *singer*, never for the sound of *ng* in finger. Examples:

bunga	*flower*
Singapura	*Singapore*
kampung	*village*

(24) NGG This combination stands for the sound of *ng* in *finger* and never for that of *ng* in *sing* or *singer*. Examples:

ringgit	*dollar*
tinggi	*tall*
tinggal	*stay*

(25) P Like English *p*, but without the puff of breath that usually accompanies English *p*. In English the Malay sound occurs after *s*. Compare the *p* of *pot* with the *p* of *spot*. Examples:

pintu	*door*
pergi	*go*
pahit	*bitter*

At the end of a word *p* is not exploded like the English *p*. When an English speaker pronounces *stop* he usually finishes up with his lips parted to allow the puff of air to come out. When a Malay says *tangkap*, however, he finishes up

with his mouth closed, the puff of air not being
allowed to emerge. Examples:

tangkap	*catch*
sedap	*tasty*

(26) R This has at least two possible pronunciations in
Malay. The English sound will not do. *r* may
either be trilled as in Scottish English (e.g.
"verra guid") or rolled in the throat as in German or French. This latter sound is more common. *r* must be pronounced at the end of a
word and not elided as in English. In the
prefixes *ber-* and *per-* the *r* is usually silent
when a consonant follows. Examples:

roti	*bread*
pagar	*fence*
berjalan	*walk (pron.* bejalan*)*
permata	*jewel (pron.* pemata*)*

(27) S Always as in *soft,* never as *z* as in *rose.* Examples:

manis	*sweet*
masam	*sour*
besar	*great (does not sound like* bazaar*)*

(28) SY Like English *sh* but made farther forward in the
mouth. This sound is not native to Malay and
occurs mainly in loan-words from English or
Arabic. The Malays frequently substitute simple
s for it. Examples:

pencen	*pension*
stesen	*station*
Syukur	*a man's name*

(29) T   Like English *t*, but without the puff of breath that usually accompanies English *t*. In English the Malay sound occurs after *s*. Compare the *t* of *top* with the *t* of *stop*. Examples:

tujuh	*seven*
timba	*bucket*
tangkap	*catch*

At the end of a word *t* is not exploded like the English *t*. The Englishman finishes a word like *pot* by taking the tip of his tongue away from the gums and allowing the air to escape. The Malay on the other hand finishes a word like *bukit* without doing this: he leaves his tongue in contact with his gums or rather the roots of his teeth and does not allow the air to escape. Examples:

bukit	*hill*
parit	*ditch*
kasut	*shoe*

(30) W   Like English *w* but a little looser. Examples:

warna	*colour*
wayang	*theatrical performance*
wak-wak	*gibbon*

(31) Y   Like English *y* in *young*. Never as *y* in *thyme* or *rhythm*, of course. Examples:

wayang	*theatrical performance*
yang	*which*
kaya	*rich*

(32) Z   Like English *z*. It occurs only in loan-words, mostly from Arabic—especially names. Exam-

ples:

Zakaria	man's name
zaman	time
muzium	museum

The Glottal Catch

The glottal catch (sometimes called the glottal stop) is the little catch in the throat that the Cockney or the Glaswegian uses in place of *t* in a word like *butter*. It also occurs in very careful speech in English in phrases like The India Office, where it is used to separate the words by people who are afraid to say The Yindia Roffice. It is a very common sound in Malay and is spelt in various ways:

(a) At the end of a word the most usual spelling is *k:*

rokok	cigarette (pron. roko')
banyak	a lot (pron. banya')
tak	not

(b) It is not indicated at all in the spelling where two *a's* come together in words like:

kemerdékaan	independence (pron. kemerdéka'an)
peperiksaan	examination (pron. peperiksa'an)
Saad	a man's name

The student should make every effort to use this glottal catch when speaking Malay. It must never be omitted, especially at the end of a word. *Banyak* must not be pronounced *banya* as if the *k* were not there, and *rokok* does not rhyme with *cocoa*. It is better to pronounce the *k* fully in these cases than to omit it altogether.

Stress

English has a very strong stress accent on each word, cf.

wínter, cóming, índepéndence. Stress in Malay, although it does exist, is not nearly so strong as in English. Indeed it is often difficult to tell on which syllable of a Malay word the stress should come; even a Malay would sometimes be hard put to it to tell you.

The strong stress of English has the effect of causing the unstressed syllables to be "swallowed," e.g. the second syllable in words like *cóuple, bóttle.* This never happens in Malay. *Kapal* does not sound in the least like *couple* for instance. Each syllable must be given its full value, the result sounding to English ears as if the stress were equal on each syllable. The stress is there, however, in the slight extra loudness given to the appropriate syllable.

Most genuine Malay words (i.e. not borrowings) have two syllables. If one of these two contains the vowel *e* then the stress falls on the other:

besár	*great*
pedás	*hot*
segán	*bashful*

When the word does not contain *e,* the stress is more usually on the first syllable although this rule is not invariable:

bányak	*a lot*
págar	*fence*
bílik	*room*

The feeling for Malay stress is better learnt by experience than by verbal description. When in doubt the student should just stress each syllable equally and then he will never be wrong.

A. Sentences

Study carefully the following sentences and their English equivalents, which are given opposite. For the moment learn each sentence as a whole; concentrate on the meaning of the whole sentence, and do not try to analyse it into separate words:

Orang itu orang Melayu.	*That man's a Malay.*
Orang itu orang Cina.	*That man's a Chinese.*
Orang itu orang India.	*That man's an Indian.*
Orang itu orang putih.	*That man's a European.*
Orang itu bukan orang Melayu; orang Cina.	*That man's not a Malay; he's a Chinese*
Orang itu bukan orang Cina; orang India.	*That man's not a Chinese; he's an Indian.*
Orang itu bukan orang India; orang putih.	*That man's not an Indian; he's a European.*
Orang itu bukan orang putih; orang Melayu.	*That man's not a European; he's a Malay.*
Orang itu orang Cina?	*Is that man a Chinese?*
Bukan; orang itu orang India.	*No, he's an Indian.*
Orang itu orang Melayu?	*Is that man a Malay?*
Orang Melayu.	*Yes, he is.*

B. Word List

bukan	*no, not*	orang	*man, person*
itu	*that, those*	Melayu	*Malay*
China	*China*	India	*India, Indian*
putih	*white*		

orang Melayu	*a Malay*
orang Cina	*a Chinese*
orang India	*an Indian*
orang putih	*a European* (lit. *a white man*)

C. *Grammar*

(1) ORANG ITU ORANG MELAYU

Notice the structure of this sentence. Basically it consists of NOUN plus NOUN, i.e. *orang* plus *orang*. After the first *orang* we put the word *itu* (that) to show which person we are talking about, i.e. that person, and after the second *orang* we place the word *Melayu* to indicate what kind of person we are talking about. However, although the sentence would make no sense without *itu* and *Melayu,* this does not alter the structure of the sentence, which remains NOUN plus NOUN. In reality *orang itu* and *orang Melayu* form NOUN-GROUPS and should be thought of as units. The real point to notice is that the verb *to be* is not used in such sentences in Malay. Although English says *that man* is *a Malay,* Malay simply says *that man Malay man.*

(2) ORANG ITU BUKAN ORANG MELAYU; ORANG CINA

Sentences of the pattern described in (1) above are negated by placing the word *bukan* between the two nouns or noun-groups or, more accurately, by placing *bukan* immediately in front of the second noun or noun-group.

Notice also the difference here in Malay and English idiom: in English we say *that man's not a Malay, he's a Chinese.* In other words we need a part of the verb *to be* (in this case *is*) in both parts of the sentence, whereas Malay needs the verb *to be* in neither part. In Malay we simply say, *that man not Malay man; Chinese man.* This simplicity of expression runs right through the language.

(3) QUESTIONS

There are several ways of forming questions from statements in Malay and during the course we shall deal with all of them. For the moment, however, let us confine ourselves to the easiest, and incidentally the commonest, way of forming them. To change *orang itu orang Melayu* (that man's a Malay) into a question all we need to do is to raise the pitch of our voice at the end of the sentence (indicated in writing by a question mark), viz. *orang itu orang Melayu?* (is that man a Malay?).

Malay idiom differs here again from English in the answers given to such questions. An example will suffice to make this clear:

Orang itu orang Melayu?	*Is that man a Malay?*
Ya, orang Melayu.	*Yes, he is.*
Bukan; orang Cina.	*No, he isn't; he's a Chinese.*

First Week   LESSON 2: TUESDAY

A. Sentences

Study carefully the following sentences and compare them with those given in Lesson 1. You will find that they follow exactly the same patterns that we have already studied.

Buah itu buah durian.	*That fruit's a durian.*
Buah itu buah limau.	*That fruit's a lime.*
Buah itu buah rambutan.	*That fruit's a rambutan.*
Buah itu buah manggis.	*That fruit's a mangosteen.*
Buah itu bukan buah durian; buah limau.	*That fruit's not a durian; it's a lime.*
Buah itu bukan buah rambutan; buah manggis.	*That fruit's not a rambutan; it's a mangosteen.*

Daging itu daging lembu.	*That meat is beef.*
Daging itu daging babi.	*That meat is pork.*
Daging itu daging kambing.	*That meat is mutton.*
Daging itu bukan daging lembu; daging babi.	*That meat is not beef; it's pork.*
Daging itu bukan daging babi; daging kambing.	*That meat is not pork; it's mutton.*

Buah itu buah manggis?	*Is that fruit a mangosteen?*
Ya, buah manggis.	*Yes, it is.*
Daging itu daging lembu?	*Is that meat beef?*
Bukan; daging babi.	*No, it isn't; it's pork.*

B. Word List

buah	*fruit*	buah manggis	*mangosteen*
buah durian	*durian*	buah limau	*lime*
buah rambutan	*rambutan*	daging	*meat, flesh*
daging lembu	*beef*	lembu	*ox, cow*
daging babi	*pork*	babi	*pig*
daging kambing	*mutton*	kambing	*goat*

C. Grammar

(4) Revise the grammar of Lesson 1.

(5) BUAH DURIAN

Notice the Malay idiom. In English it is enough to give the name of the fruit—apple, pear, banana, etc.—but, although we can do this in Malay, too, it is better Malay to use the word *buah* (fruit) as well. This idiom of using a generic term followed by some word indicating a more specific meaning is very common in Malay. We see it again in the use of the word *daging* in such expressions *daging lembu,* beef.

First Week

A. Sentences

Orang Melayu itu makan nasi.	*That Malay eats rice.*
Orang Cina itu makan daging babi.	*That Chinese eats pork.*
Orang India itu makan daging kambing.	*That Indian eats mutton.*
Orang putih itu makan daging lembu.	*That European eats beef.*
Orang putih itu tidak makan buah durian.	*That European does not eat durians.*
Orang Melayu tidak makan daging babi.	*Malays do not eat pork.*
Orang India itu tidak makan daging lembu.	*That Indian does not eat beef.*
Orang putih itu makan daging lembu?	*Does that European eat beef?*
Makan.	*Yes, he does.*
Orang Melayu itu makan daging babi?	*Does that Malay eat pork?*
Tidak; makan daging kambing.	*No, he doesn't; he eats mutton.*
Orang India itu makan daging kambing?	*Does that Indian eat mutton?*
Makan.	*Yes, he does.*
Orang putih itu makan buah durian?	*Does that European eat durians?*
Tidak, makan buah rambutan.	*No, he doesn't; he eats rambutans.*

B. Word List

makan	*eat*
nasi	*(cooked) rice*
tidak	*no, not, don't, doesn't*

C. Grammar

(6) ORANG MELAYU ITU MAKAN NASI

Here we have a new sentence pattern, viz. NOUN-GROUP plus VERB plus NOUN-GROUP, in which the first NOUN OR NOUN-GROUP is the subject of the verb which follows it, and the final NOUN or NOUN-GROUP is the object of that verb. Such sentences are, of course, equally common in English.

(7) ORANG PUTIH ITU TIDAK MAKAN BUAH DURIAN

Sentences of the pattern explained in (6) above are negated by placing the word *tidak* (not) in front of the verb. The English construction with the verb *to do* (e.g. I do not come, etc.) is quite foreign to Malay. In colloquial speech *tidak* is usually pronounced *tak*, except in answer to questions and when standing by itself with the meaning "no," when it is usually pronounced in full as *tidak*. The spelling and pronunciation *tidak* are always correct.

(8) ORANG MELAYU TIDAK MAKAN DAGING BABI

Notice that Malay makes no distinction between singular and plural.

(9) Malay verbs make no distinction in form between singular and plural, neither do they change for person or tense.

(10) ORANG PUTIH ITU

Notice the order of the words making up this noun-group; it is the reverse of the English order. From this we can deduce the rule that in Malay adjectives follow their nouns, and words like *itu* come last of all.

A. Sentences

Orang itu orang Cina.	*That man's a Chinese.*
Dia baca buku.	*He's reading a book.*
Dia baca buku Cina.	*He's reading a Chinese book.*
Dia tidak baca buku Melayu.	*He's not reading a Malay book.*
Orang putih itu tulis surat.	*That European's writing a letter.*
Dia tidak baca buku.	*He isn't reading a book.*
Orang Melayu itu baca suratkhabar.	*That Malay is reading the newspaper.*
Dia baca suratkhabar Melayu.	*He's reading a Malay newspaper.*
Dia tidak baca suratkhabar Cina.	*He's not reading a Chinese newspaper.*
Orang India itu jual suratkhabar.	*That Indian sells newspapers.*
Dia jual buku.	*He sells books.*
Dia tidak jual daging	*He doesn't sell meat.*
Orang Melayu itu beli apa?	*What is that Malay buying?*
Dia beli suratkhabar.	*He's buying a newspaper.*
Orang Cina itu jual apa?	*What does that Chinese sell?*
Dia jual daging babi.	*He sells pork.*

B. Word List

dia	*he, she*	baca	*read*
buku	*book*	tulis	*write*
surat	*letter*	khabar	*news*
suratkhabar	*newspaper*	jual	*sell*
beli	*buy*	apa	*what*

C. Grammar

(11) Revise the grammar of Lesson 3.

(12) ORANG MELAYU ITU BELI APA?

Notice the order of words. Although this is a question, it still keeps to the sentence pattern studied in (6) above, i.e. SUBJECT + VERB + OBJECT. Actually, in this case the English order is also possible— *apa orang Melayu itu beli?*

First Week   LESSON 5: FRIDAY

A. Sentences

Orang itu orang laki-laki.	*That person is a man.*
Orang ini orang perempuan.	*This person is a woman.*
Budak itu budak laki-laki.	*That youngster is a boy.*
Budak ini budak perempuan.	*This youngster is a girl.*

Budak laki-laki Cina ini makan daging babi.	*This Chinese boy is eating pork.*
Dia tidak makan nasi.	*He's not eating rice.*
Di mana dia beli daging babi itu?	*Where did he buy that pork?*
Dia beli di kedai Cina.	*He bought it in a Chinese shop.*
Di mana kedai Cina itu?	*Where is that Chinese shop?*
Kedai itu di pasar Cina.	*That shop is in the Chinese market.*
Pasar itu pasar Melayu.	*That market is a Malay market.*
Bukan. Pasar itu pasar Cina.	*No, it isn't. That market is a Chinese market.*
Kedai itu kedai Cina.	*That shop's a Chinese shop.*
Bukan. Kedai itu kedai India.	*No, it isn't. That shop's an Indian shop.*

Orang India itu jual buku dan suratkhabar.	*That Indian sells books and newspapers.*
Orang Cina ini beli daging babi dan buah rambutan.	*This Chinese is buying pork and rambutans.*

B. Word List

laki-laki	*male*	perempuan	*female*
budak	*youngster, child*	di mana	*where*
di	*in, at*	kedai	*shop*
pasar	*market, bazaar*	dan	*and*
ini	*this, these*	mana	*which*

C. Grammar

(13) BUDAK LAKI-LAKI; BUDAK PEREMPUAN

As we have seen Malay does not usually bother to distinguish grammatically between the sexes, e.g. *dia* means either *he* or *she*. Similarly *budak* may mean either *boy* or *girl* and usually the context will be sufficient to tell us which is meant. The same applies to *orang* (which can mean *man* or *woman*, hence *person*) and many other words. If, for any reason, it becomes important to specify the sex then the words *laki-laki* (male) and *perempuan* (female) are added after the word whose sex is in question. *Laki-laki* and *perempuan* are used only, however, to refer to human beings. To distinguish the sex of animals the word *jantan* (male) and *betina* (female) are used in the same way. Colloquially, *jantan* is sometimes used instead of *laki-laki*, but the beginner had better avoid this use for fear of giving offence if he uses it in the wrong place.

(14) DI KEDAI

Di is a preposition and precedes the word which it governs. It corresponds to various English prepositions according to context, but most commonly it is equivalent to *in* or *at*.

(15) Notice that Malay does not normally have equivalents for English *a* or *an* or *the*. There **are** ways of rendering these English words, but we shall leave them until later. *Kedai*, therefore, may mean *shop, a shop, shops, the shop,* or *the shops*.

(16) DI MANA KEDAI CINA ITU?

Notice that the verb *to be* is not required in such sentences as this in Malay.

First Week   REVISION LESSON A: WEEK-END

A. Sentences

Revise all the sentences in Lessons 1–5.

B. Word List

Revise all the word lists in Lessons 1–5.

C. Grammar

Revise all the grammar sections (1–16) in Lessons 1–5.

D. Exercises

(1) Make up twenty sentences using the words and sentence patterns you have so far learnt.

(2) Read the following conversation aloud, and then translate into English:

DI PASAR

A. Pasar ini pasar Melayu?

B. Bukan; pasar Cina.

A. Orang itu orang Cina?

B. Orang Cina.

A. Apa dia jual?

B. Dia jual daging.

A. Daging apa dia jual?

B. Daging babi, daging lembu dan daging kambing.

A. Di mana dia jual daging itu?

B. Di kedai.

A. Apa orang ini jual di kedai ini?

B. Dia jual buku dan suratkhabar.

A. Buku dan suratkhabar Melayu?

B. Tidak. Dia orang Cina. Dia jual buku dan suratkhabar Cina.

(3) Translate into Malay:
   (a) What does he sell in that shop?
   (b) That girl is a Chinese.
   (c) This boy is a European.
   (d) This Indian girl eats rice and mutton.
   (e) Where is that shop?
   (f) What is that Chinese boy writing?
   (g) He is writing a letter.
   (h) Where does he buy pork?
   (i) That woman is a Malay.
   (j) That Malay woman is buying mutton in that shop.

A. Sentences

Budak ini anak orang Cina itu.	*This boy is the son of that Chinese.*
Dia bukan anak orang India ini.	*He is not this Indian's son.*
Rumah ini rumah orang putih itu.	*This house is that European's.*
Rumah ini bukan rumah orang Melayu ini.	*This house is not this Malay's.*
Di mana rumah orang itu?	*Where is that man's house?*
Rumah dia di pasar Cina.	*His house is in the Chinese market.*
Bangunan ini bangunan apa?	*What is this building?*
Bangunan ini hospital.	*This building is the hospital.*
Orang India itu sakit.	*That Indian is ill.*
Orang Cina itu tidak sakit.	*That Chinese is not ill.*
Anak orang itu sakit.	*That man's son is ill.*
Dia di hospital.	*He's in hospital.*
Ini keréta lembu.	*This is a bullock cart.*
Itu kerétapi.	*That is a train.*
Keréta orang Melayu itu keréta besar.	*That Malay's car is a big one.*
Ini bukan keréta lembu; kerétapi.	*This is not a bullock cart; it's a train.*

B. Word List

anak	*child, offspring, son, daughter*	anak laki-laki	*son*
		anak perém-puan	*daughter*
rumah	*house*	sakit	*ill*
hospital	*hospital*	keréta	*vehicle, car, cart*
keréta lembu	*bullock cart*		
kerétapi	*train*	api	*fire*
		bangunan	*building*

C. Grammar

(17) ANAK ORANG CINA ITU

Possession, which in English is indicated by an apostrophe s, by the use of the word *of* or the use of a possessive adjective such as *my, your, his,* etc., is expressed in Malay simply by placing the person or thing possessed in front of the possessor. Examples:

> anak dia   *his son*
> buku orang itu   *that man's books*
> kedai orang ini   *this man's shop*

(18) KERÉTAPI

A similar construction to that in (17) above is used to form compound words, which are very common in Malay. Examples:

> kerétapi   *train* (lit. *vehicle of fire*)
> (= keréta + api)
> keréta lembu   *bullock cart*
> suratkhabar   *newspaper*

Note that in the case of compound words the word-order is the reverse of that used in English, and that in the modern spelling such compounds are usually written together as one word.

Second Week LESSON 7: TUESDAY

A. Sentences

Apa khabar?	*How are you?*
Khabar baik, terima kasih.	*I'm very well, thank you.*
Saya orang Melayu.	*I'm a Malay.*
Saya tidak makan daging babi.	*I don't eat pork.*
Anak saya tidak makan daging babi.	*My son doesn't eat pork.*
Bapa saya tidak makan daging babi.	*My father doesn't eat pork.*
Emak saya tidak makan daging babi.	*My mother doesn't eat pork.*
Kami makan daging lembu dan daging kambing.	*We eat beef and mutton.*
Encik orang Melayu?	*Are you a Malay?*
Bukan. Saya orang Cina.	*No, I'm a Chinese.*
Apa encik makan?	*What do you eat?*
Saya makan daging babi.	*I eat pork.*
Apa orang Melayu itu makan?	*What is that Malay eating?*
Dia makan buah durian.	*He is eating a durian.*
Apa orang India itu makan?	*What's that Indian eating?*
Dia makan buah manggis.	*He's eating a mangosteen.*
Apa orang putih itu makan?	*What's that European eating?*
Dia makan daging lembu.	*He's eating beef.*

B. Word List

baik	*good*	saya	*I, me*
bapa	*father*	emak	*mother*
*kami, kita	*us, we*	encik	*you, sir, Mr.*

*kami: "we/us," *excluding* the person addressed (i.e. "we but not you")
kita: "we/us," *including* the person addressed (i.e. "we (or I) and you")
In good Malay these two words are carefully distinguished.

C. Grammar

(19) APA KHABAR?

Literally this means *What is the news?* The correct answer is *Khabar baik,* literally *the news is good.* You should say this even if the news is not good at all, but simply terrible! These two expressions are the most common of all Malay greetings, and can be used at any time of the day or night. They are therefore equivalent to the English *good morning, good afternoon* and *good evening.*

Nowadays, however, the following additional phrases are very widely used and should also be known:

Selamat pagi!	*Good morning!*
Selamat tengahari!	*Good day!* [Used between about 11.00 a.m. and 1.00 p.m.]
Selamat petang!	*Good afternoon! Good evening! [before dark.]*
Selamat malam!	*Good evening!* [after dark]
Selamat tidur!	*Good night!* [Said at bedtime]

Note also:

Selamat datang!	*Welcome!*

(20) ANAK SAYA

My son. This is the same construction as (17) in Lesson 6, q.v.

(21) Revise the grammar of Lesson 6.

Second Week   LESSON 8: WEDNESDAY

A. Sentences

Selamat malam, Encik Zainal?	*Good evening, Mr Zainal.*
Selamat malam encik.	*Good evening sir.*

Di pasar Cina ini ada kedai makan.	*In this Chinese market there is a restaurant.*
Di kedai makan itu ada orang makan.	*In the restaurant there are people eating.*
Di pasar Melayu ada orang jual buah.	*In the Malay market are people selling fruit.*
Di Kuala Lumpur ada hospital.	*In Kuala Lumpur there's a hospital.*
Di hospital itu ada orang sakit.	*In the hospital there are sick people* (or: *patients*).
Bapa saya ada di Kuala Lumpur.	*My father is in Kuala Lumpur.*
Emak saya ada di Batu Pahat.	*My mother is in Batu Pahat.*
Anak saya ada di Seremban.	*My son is in Seremban.*

Saya ada rumah di kampung Melayu.	*I've got a house in the Malay village.*
Dia ada kedai di pasar Cina.	*He's got a shop in the Chinese market.*
Encik ada keréta?	*Have you got a car?*
Ada.	*Yes, I have.*
Bapa encik ada keréta?	*Has your father got a car?*
Tidak ada.	*No, he hasn't.*
Bapa saya ada basikal.	*My father's got a bicycle.*

B. Word List

kedai makan	*restaurant*	ada	*to be; to exist; to have*
orang sakit	*patient* (n.)		
basikal	*bicycle*		
kampung	*village*		

C. Grammar

(22) ADA

The word *ada* has two principal uses:

(a) To express existence in a place:

Di pasar Cina ada kedai makan.
In the Chinese market there is a restaurant.

Bapa saya ada di Kuala Lumpur.
My father is in Kuala Lumpur.

(b) To express possession:

Saya ada rumah di kampung Melayu.
I've got a house in the Malay village.

Bapa saya ada basikal.
My father's got a bicycle.

(23) ADA ORANG MAKAN

There are people eating. Although English must have the present participle in such a sentence (viz. eat*ing*), the simple verb is enough in Malay.

Second Week   LESSON 9: THURSDAY

A. Sentences

Di pasar Melayu ada kedai kopi.	*In the Malay market is a coffee shop.*
Di kedai kopi itu ada ramai orang Melayu.	*In the coffee shop are a lot of Malays.*
Orang Melayu itu makan nasi.	*They are eating rice.*
Ada ramai orang Melayu minum kopi.	*There are a lot of Malays drinking coffee.*
Orang Melayu itu bercakap Melayu.	*They are speaking Malay.*

Di pasar Cina ada kedai makan.	In the Chinese market is a restaurant.
Di kedai makan itu ada ramai orang Cina.	In the restaurant are a lot of Chinese.
Orang Cina itu tidak makan nasi; makan daging babi.	They're not eating rice; they're eating pork.
Ada ramai orang Cina minum teh.	There are a lot of Chinese drinking tea.
Orang Cina it bercakap bahasa Cina.	They're speaking Chinese.

Orang India itu bercakap bahasa Tamil.	That Indian speaks Tamil.
Dia tidak bercakap bahasa Inggeris.	He doesn't speak English.
Apa dia makan?	What's he eating?
Dia makan daging kambing.	He's eating mutton.
Apa dia minum?	What's he drinking?
Dia minum air.	He's drinking water.
Selamat tinggal!	Good-bye!
Selamat jalan, encik!	Good-bye, sir!

B. Word List

kopi	coffee	kedai kopi	coffee-shop, café
ramai	a lot; much, many	minum	to drink
bercakap	speak	bahasa	language
bahasa Melayu	Malay	bahasa Cina	Chinese
bahasa Tamil	Tamil	bahasa Inggeris	English language
Inggeris	English		
teh	tea	air	water
selamat	peace, safety	tinggal	stay, remain
jalan	road, way		

C. Grammar

(24) BERCAKAP MELAYU/BERCAKAP BAHASA CINA

Malays usually leave out the word *bahasa* after *bercakap* when referring to their own language. With the names of other languages, however, the generic term *bahasa* is usually retained. Thus we should say:

saya bercakap Melayu	*I speak Malay*

BUT

saya bercakap bahasa Malaysia	*I speak* [the] *Malaysian* [language]
saya bercakap bahasa Inggeris	*I speak English*

and so on.

(25) RAMAI and BANYAK

Both these words are used where English would use *much* or *many*. Unlike the English words, they are not truly adjectives, but should be considered rather as nouns: *ramai* means "crowd[s]" and *banyak* means "a lot". Both words precede the noun they 'qualify'.

Examples

ramai orang Cina	*many Chinese* or *a lot of Chinese*
ramai orang perempuan	*many women*
ramai budak laki-laki	*many boys*
banyak kucing	*many cats*
banyak basikal	*many bicycles* or *a lot of bicycles*
banyak suratkhabar	*many newspapers*
banyak nasi	*much rice* or *a lot of rice*
Notice the difference between ramai orang	*lots of people* [lit. "a crowd of people"]

and

orangramai   *the [general] public* [lit. "the
                               people in/of the crowd"]

(26) SELAMAT TINGGAL: SELAMAT JALAN

This is the commonest leave-taking formula in Malay.
The person going away says *selamat tinggal*, which means
peace be on your staying or *remain in peace;* the person
staying behind says *selamat jalan* which means *peace be on
your road* or *go in peace.*

(27) ENCIK

We have already had this word with the meaning *you.*
This, however, is not its real meaning. *Encik* is the commonest Malay title and corresponds to the English *Mr* or
Sir. Malays, however, do not like using the second-person
pronoun *you* and prefer to call people either by their names
or by their titles. Hence *encik* often corresponds to *you* in
English, and, for the moment at least, you will be quite
safe if you use it when addressing a strange Malay.

Second , Week   LESSON 10: FRIDAY

A. Sentences

Siapa nama orang itu?	*What is the man's name?*
Nama dia Abdullah. .	*His name's Abdullah.*
Dia orang Melayu.	*He's a Malay.*
Dia bercakap Melayu.	*He speaks Malay.*
Dia tak tahu bahasa Tamil.	*He doesn't know Tamil.*

Siapa nama orang itu?	*What is that man's name?*
Nama dia Krishna.	*His name's Krishna.*
Dia orang India.	*He's an Indian.*

Dia bercakap bahasa Tamil. *He speaks Tamil.*
Dia tak tahu bahasa Inggeris. *He doesn't know English.*

Apa orang itu buat?	*What is that man doing?*
Dia makan nasi.	*He's eating.*
Dia duduk di kedai makan nasi.	*He's sitting in the restaurant eating.*
Apa dia minum?	*What's he drinking?*
Dia minum teh.	*He's drinking tea.*

Siapa nama encik?	*What's your name?*
Nama saya Abdul Rahman.	*My name's Abdul Rahman.*

B. Word List

siapa	*who*	nama	*name*
tahu	*know*	buat	*do, make*
duduk	*sit*		

C. Grammar

(28) SIAPA NAMA ORANG ITU?

Notice the Malay idiom: *who* is the name of that man? It is also correct to say *apa nama orang itu?* but the form with *siapa* is considered more polite.

(29) DIA MAKAN NASI

Notice that I have translated this by *he's eating* and not *he's eating rice.* In Malay it is very rare to use a word like *makan* by itself without an object. If the man is eating, he must be eating something, and if he is a Malay the chances are that his meal consists of rice. *Makan nasi* has, in other words, become a set expression for *having a meal* and is used by Malays even when the meal does not contain rice. This will not seem at all strange to Chinese students who say just the same thing in Chinese (Mandarin: chi-fan; Cantonese sik-faan).

Second Week REVISION LESSON B: WEEK-END

A. Sentences

Revise all the sentences in Lessons 6–10.

B. Word List

Revise all the word lists in Lessons 6–10.

C. Grammar

Revise all the grammar sections (17–29) in Lessons 6–10.

D. Exercises

(1) Make up twenty sentences using the words and sentence patterns you have so far learnt.

(2) Read aloud the following conversation, which takes place outside a restaurant:

A. Apa khabar?
B. Khabar baik.

A. Di mana ada kedai makan Melayu?
B. Di pasar Melayu ada kedai makan Melayu.

A. Ada ramai orang di kedai itu?
B. Ada. Ada ramai orang Melayu di kedai itu.

A. Apa orang itu makan?
B. Di kedai itu ada orang makan nasi, ada orang makan daging kambing, dan ada orang makan daging lembu.

A. Apa orang minum di kedai makan itu?
B. Ada orang minum teh, ada orang minum kopi, dan ada orang minum air.

A. Ada orang makan buah?
B. Ada.

A. Buah apa orang makan di kedai itu?
B. Ada orang makan buah durian, ada orang makan buah manggis, dan ada orang makan buah rambutan.

A. Selamat tinggal!
B. Selamat jalan!

(3) Translate the conversation in (2) into English.
(4) Translate into Malay:
    (a) What's your name?
    (b) My name is Ah Chong. I'm a Chinese.
    (c) Do you eat pork? Yes, I do.
    (d) Do you eat beef? No, I'm an Indian; Indians don't eat beef.
    (e) What does that Chinese sell?
    (f) He sells books and newspapers.
    (g) Where is your father? My father is in Kuala Lumpur.
    (h) Has your son got a car? No, He hasn't.
    (i) I've got a bicycle. I haven't got a car.
    (j) That Malay's got a bullock cart.

A. Sentences

Orang putih itu suka makan nasi.	*That European likes eating rice.*
Orang putih ini tidak suka makan nasi.	*This European does not like eating rice.*
Orang India itu mahu makan nasi.	*That Indian wants to eat rice.*
Orang Cina ini tidak mahu makan nasi.	*This Chinese does not to eat rice.*
Orang Cina boléh makan daging babi.	*Chinese can eat pork.*
Orang Melayu tidak boléh makan daging babi.	*Malays cannot eat it.*
Saya suka minum téh.	*I like drinking tea.*
Saya tak suka minum kopi.	*I don't like drinking coffee.*
Dia mahu minum air.	*He wants to drink water.*
Dia tak mahu minum téh.	*He doesn't want to drink tea.*
Dia tahu bercakap bahasa Inggeris.	*He knows how to speak English.*
Saya tak tahu bercakap bahasa Cina.	*I don't know how to speak Chinese.*
Di pasar saya tak boléh beli buah durian; buah durian tak ada.	*In the market I couldn't buy any durians; there weren't any.*
Buah manggis ada; encik boléh beli buah manggis.	*There were some mangosteens; you could have bought some of those.*
Orang itu tidak suka makan buah durian.	*That man doesn't like eating durians.*
Dia orang putih; ramai orang putih tidak	*He's a European; a lot of Europeans don't like*

suka makan buah durian.	*eating durians.*
Siapa suka makan buah durian?	*Who likes eating durians?*
Orang Melayu suka makan buah durian.	*The Malays do.*
Saya tak boléh duduk di Kuala Lumpur; saya tak ada rumah.	*I can't stay in Kuala Lumpur; I haven't got a house.*

B. Word List

suka	*like*	mahu	*want*
boléh	*can, be able*	tahu	*know (a fact); know*
duduk	*sit, stay, live, dwell*		*how to*

C. Grammar

(30) SUKA MAKAN

Here we have two verbs dependent on one another. In English we have various ways of connecting two verbs together. Examples:

> he likes eat*ing*
> he can eat
> he wants *to* eat

In Malay, however, the process is much easier: all we have to do is to place the verbs side by side without any alteration in form and without the insertion of a preposition. (Cf. the other sentences in Section A of this lesson, containing the words *suka, mahu, boléh,* and *tahu.*)

(31) BAHASA INGGERIS

This is the correct expression for *English* [language]. Quite often, however, especially in country districts, you may hear the phrase *bahasa orang putih* [lit. "white man's language."]

(32) DI PASAR SAYA TAK BOLÉH BELI BUAH DURIAN

Remember what you were told in Grammar Section (9): there are no distinctions of tense or mood in Malay. It depends entirely on the context of the Malay sentence and which tense we use to translate it in English. Cf. also *ençik boléh beli buah manggis* which in this context requires the conditional perfect in English: you could have bought, etc.

(33) DUDUK

We have already had this word in its basic meaning of *sit* or *sit down*. It also means *stay* in the sense of staying in a hotel, for instance; not *stay* in the sense of staying behind, which is *tinggal*. *Duduk* also means *to live* in the sense of *to dwell*, not in the sense of *being alive*, which is *hidup*.

Third Week   LESSON 12: TUESDAY

A. Sentences

Semalam saya mahu beli buah durian di pasar.
Yesterday I wanted to buy some durians in the market.

Buah durian tak ada semalam.
There weren't any durians yesterday.

Saya tak dapat beli.
I didn't manage to buy any.

Hari ini saya cari buah durian.
Today I looked for durians.

Hari ini ada buah durian.
Today there were some durians.

Saya dapat beli.
I managed to buy some.

Bésok saya mahu beli ikan dan daging di pasar.
Tomorrow I shall want to buy fish and meat in the market.

Apa encik mahu beli semalam di pasar?
What did you want to buy yesterday in the market?

Saya mahu beli ikan.	*I wanted to buy fish.*
Encik dapat?	*Did you get any?*
Dapat.	*Yes, I did.*
Encik cuba beli buah manggis semalam?	*Did you try to buy mangosteens yesterday?*
Cuba; buah manggis tak ada semalam.	*Yes, I did; (but) there weren't any mangosteens yesterday.*
Encik tahu bercakap bahasa Cina?	*Can you speak Chinese?*
Tidak; saya tak tahu.	*No, I can't.*
Encik tak boléh makan di kedai makan Cina itu.	*You can't eat in that Chinese restaurant.*
Orang kedai itu orang Cina.	*The man in that shop's a Chinese (or: the shop-keeper's a Chinese).*
Dia tak tahu bercakap Melayu.	*He can't speak Malay.*
Terima kasih.	*Thank you very much indeed.*
Baiklah.	*All right (or: O.K.).*

B. Word List

semalam	*yesterday*	hari ini	*today*
bésok	*tomorrow*	dapat	*get, receive, obtain; manage*
cari	*seek, look for*		
cuba	*try*	ikan	*fish*
terima	*receive*	orang kedai	*shopkeeper*
lah	*emphatic particle*	kasih	*love* (n.)
terima kasih	*thank you very much indeed*	baiklah	*all right, O.K.*
		hari	*day*

C. Grammar

(34) Revise the grammar of Lesson 11.

(35) HARI INI

Literally, *this day*.

(36) TERIMA KASIH

Literally, *receive (my) love*. This expression is used much less by Malays than the English *thank you*. Strictly speaking it should be used only to thank someone for a very special favour. Malays indicate thanks more often with a gesture or a smile than with words. *Baiklah* is often used where we would use *thank you*, in thanking a servant for bringing or doing something, for example. However, the use of *terima kasih* is on the increase, especially among Malays who know English, so it will do no harm for the non-Malay to use it where he would say *thank you* in his own language.

(37) BAIKLAH

lah added to a word emphasises it, so that *baiklah* means something like *very good*, and like the English *very good* (cf. the military *very good, Sir*) it has come to mean *all right*, or *O.K.*

Third Week

LESSON 13: WEDNESDAY

A. Sentences

Saya pergi ke Kuala Lumpur.	*I'm going to Kuala Lumpur.*
Saya datang dari Kuala Kangsar.	*I come from Kuala Kangsar.*
Semalam saya datang dari Alor Setar.	*Yesterday I came from Alor Star.*
Hari ini saya duduk di Ipoh.	*Today I am staying in Ipoh.*
Bésok saya pergi ke Kuala Lumpur.	*Tomorrow I am going to Kuala Lumpur.*

Semalam Osman pergi ke pasar; dia mahu beli ikan.	*Yesterday Osman went to the market; he wanted to buy fish.*
Semalam ikan tak ada di pasar.	*Yesterday there wasn't any fish in the market.*
Osman datang dari pasar ke rumah saya.	*Osman came from the market to my house.*
Saya tak ada ikan; Osman tak dapat beli.	*I didn't have any fish; so Osman didn't manage to buy any.*
Saya beri surat kepada dia.	*I give a letter to him (or: I give him a letter).*
Saya dapat (*or:* terima) surat daripada dia.	*I get (or: receive) a letter from him.*
Bésok saya ada ikan.	*Tomorrow I shall have some fish.*
Saya beri ikan itu kepada Osman.	*I'll give the fish to Osman.*
Osman dapat ikan itu daripada saya.	*Osman will get the fish from me.*
Semalam saya dapat surat daripada anak saya di Raub.	*Yesterday I got a letter from my daughter in Raub.*
Hari ini saya tulis surat kepada bapa saya di Melaka.	*Today I wrote a letter to my father in Malacca.*
Bapa saya mahu pergi ke Kuala Lipis.	*My father wants to go to Kuala Lipis.*
Dia tak ada keréta; tak boléh pergi hari ini.	*He hasn't got a car; so he can't go today.*
Dari mana encik datang semalam?	*Where did you come from yesterday?*
Semalam saya datang dari Kota Baharu.	*Yesterday I came from Kota Bharu.*

B. Word List

pergi	*go*	datang	*come*
ke	*to*	dari	*from*
kepada	*to*	daripada	*from*
Alor Setar	*Alor Star*	beri	*give*
Melaka	*Malacca*	dari	*where. . . . from;*
Kota Baharu	*Kota Bharu*	mana	*from where; whence*

C. Grammar

(34a) KE and KEPADA

Both these words mean *to*. *Ke* is used before names of places, and *kepada* before words indicating people or animals.

(35a) DARI and DARIPADA

Both these words mean *from*. The difference is the same as that between *ke* and *kepada*, i.e. *dari* is used before places and *daripada before people and animals.*

(36a) ALOR SETAR, MELAKA, KOTA BAHARU

Notice the difference in spelling between English and Malay. In practice, however, Alor Star and Kota Bharu usually keep the English spelling even in Malay texts. For the time being the student should stick to the more correct Malay spelling.

(37a) PERGI

Usually pronounced *pegi* in careful speech. The -r- is pronounced normally only in excessively careful speech, such as might be used on very formal occasions, e.g. in the mosque. In rapid colloquial speech *pergi* is pronounced either *pi* or *gi*.

(38) BÉSOK

Another, equally common, form of this word is *ésok*. Both mean "tomorrow".

Third Week

LESSON 14: THURSDAY

A. Sentences

Dia naik keréta.	*He travels by car.*
Saya naik basikal	*I ride a bicycle.*
Bapa dia naik béca.	*His father rides in a trishaw.*
Orang itu naik kapal.	*That man travels by ship.*
Kita naik kerétapi.	*We are travelling by train.*
Dia naik keréta pergi ke Alor Setar.	*He goes to Alor Setar by car.*
Dia naik beca pergi ke hospital.	*He goes to the hospital by trishaw.*
Dia naik kapal pergi ke Singapura.	*She goes to Singapore by ship.*
Baik kita bercakàp Melayu.	*We had better speak Malay.*
Baik dia tulis surat kepada anak dia.	*He'd better write a letter to his son.*
Béca! Mari ke sini!	*Trishaw! Come here!*
Encik mahu pergi ke mana?	*Where do you want to go to?*
Saya mahu pergi ke pasar Melayu.	*I want to go to the Malay market.*
Dari sana saya mahu pergi ke hospital.	*From there I want to go to the hospital.*
Baiklah, encik. Encik boléh naik béca saya pergi ke sana.	*All right, sir, You can go there in my trishaw.*
Orang itu tak tahu tulis.	*That man doesn't know how to write.*
Orang ini tak tahu	*This man doesn't know how*

baca.	*to read.*
Beri surat ini kepada emak dia.	*Give this letter to his mother.*
Tulis surat kepada bapa encik.	*Write a letter to your father.*
Emak saya tak suka naik basikal.	*My mother doesn't like riding a bicycle.*
Dia suka naik keréta.	*She likes travelling by car.*

B. Word List

naik	*go up; ascend; mount; travel by; ride (in, on)*		
béca	*trishaw; rickshaw*	kapal	*ship*
Singapura	*Singapore*	baik	*had better,* (39)
mari!	*come! (imperative)*	ke sini	*(to) here; hither*
ke mana	*where . . . . to; whither*	dari sana	*from there; thence*
		ke sana	*(to) there; thither*

C. Grammar

(39) BAIK KITA BERCAKAP MELAYU

Notice this use of *baik*. When prefixed to a sentence like this it corresponds in meaning to the English expressions *had better, it wouldn't be a bad idea if,* etc.

(40) NAIK KERETA

The basic meaning of *naik* is *go up, ascend*. From this meaning comes (as in the case of *monter* in French) the derived meaning of getting into or on to some conveyance or other, hence *to ride* or *to travel*. The examples in Section A of this lesson should give a sufficient idea of the variety of translations *naik* may have in English.

(41) MARI

Datang is the only Malay verb with a special form for the imperative mood. (The mood used to give orders and commands.) Normally we simply use the plain form of the verb, e.g. *tulis surat,* write a letter. *Datang,* however, is not usually used like this, *mari* being used instead. In colloquial speech, especially in North Malay, *mari* is used entirely in place of *datang,* which sounds a bit bookish. Nevertheless, the student is advised to reserve *mari* for giving orders, and *datang* for all other cases.

Third Week   LESSON 15: FRIDAY

A. Sentences

Saya mahu pergi ke hospital téngok bapa saya.	*I want to go to the hospital to see my father.*
Di Kuala Lumpur ada banyak panggung wayang gambar.	*In Kuala Lumpur there are many cinemas.*
Saya mahu pergi ke Kuala Lumpur téngok wayang gambar.	*I want to go to Kuala Lumpur to go to the cinema.*
Bésok saya balik dari Kuala Lumpur.	*Tomorrow I shall return from Kuala Lumpur.*
Saya naik kerétapi balik dari Singapura ke-Johor Baharu.	*I returned from Singapore to Johore Bahru by train.*
Saya belajar bahasa Melayu.	*I am learning Malay.*
Bésok bapa saya mulai belajar bahasa Melayu.	*Tomorrow my father will begin to learn Malay.*
Orang Cina itu tahu bercakap Melayu?	*Does that Chinese know how to speak Malay?*
Tidak; dia mulai belajar hari ini.	*No, he's beginning to learn today.*
Saya mahu belajar bahasa Cina dan bahasa Tamil.	*I want to learn Chinese and Tamil.*

Baik encik pergi ke Kuala Lumpur belajar di sana.	*You'd better go to Kuala Lumpur to learn them there.*
Encik ada keréta?	*Have you got a car?*
Ada; saya naik keréta pergi ke Kuala Lumpur.	*Yes, I have; I'll go to Kuala Lumpur by car.*
Di mana saya boléh beli keréta?	*Where can I buy a car?*
Baik encik pergi ke Singapura; di sana boléh beli.	*You'd better go to Singapore; you can buy one there.*
Bapa dia balik dari Kuala Lumpur bésok.	*His father is coming back from Kuala Lumpur tomorrow.*
Macam mana dia balik ke sini?	*How is he coming back here?*
Dia naik kerétapi balik ke sini.	*He's coming back here by train.*

B. Word List

téngok	*look at, see, watch*	panggung	*theatre, stage*
gambar	*picture*	wayang	*theatrical performance*
balik	*return, go back, come back*	wayang gambar	*film*
		Johor Baharu	*Johore Bahru*
belajar	*learn*	mulaï	*begin*
di sana	*there*		

C. Grammar

(42) TÉNGOK

This word basically means *look at*, i.e. *see with deliberation* as in the case of seeing a film or a play. *See* in the sense of *catch sight of* or *see without conscious effort* is *nampak* in Malay. Examples:

Saya nampak dia beli ikan.

I saw him buy fish (i.e. because I just happened to be there and look in his direction).

Saya téngok dia beli ikan.

I saw (i.e. watched) him buy fish.

(43) DIA NAIK APA BALIK KE SINI?

Notice the construction—*he mounting-what return hither?* Notice too how the construction is mirrored in the reply: *dia naik kerétapi balik ke sini,* i.e. *he mounting-train return hither.*

Third Week   REVISION LESSON C: WEEK-END

A. Sentences

Revise all the sentences in Lessons 11–15.

B. Word List

Revise all the word lists in Lessons 11–15.

C. Grammar

Revise all the grammar sections (30–43) in Lessons 11–15.

D. Exercises

(1) Make up thirty sentences using the words and sentence patterns you have already learnt.

(2) Read aloud the following conversation between a trishaw pedaller and his customer:

A. Béca! Mari ke sini!

B. Baiklah encik. Encik mahu pergi ke mana?

A. Saya mahu pergi ke Kuala Lumpur. Saya mahu téngok wayang gambar di sana.

B. Baiklah, encik. Baik naik béca saya.

(Later)

B. Baiklah, encik. Di sini panggung wayang gambar (*Di sini,* here.)

A. Baiklah. Terima kasih. Selamat jalan.

B. Selamat tinggal, encik.

(3) Translate the conversation in (2) into English.

(4) Translate into Malay:

   (a) How do you want to go to Singapore?

   (b) I want to go by train.

   (c) Don't you want to go by car?

   (d) No, I don't. I don't like travelling by car.

   (e) My father returned from my mother's house in Raub today.

   (f) This Malay boy wants to learn Chinese.

   (g) He'd better go to Kuala Lumpur and learn it there.

   (h) My mother began to learn Tamil yesterday.

   (i) Can you speak English? No, I can't.

   (j) I went to Singapore yesterday to buy a car (but) I couldn't get one.

   (k) Write that Chinese a letter.

   (l) I received a letter from my mother today.

  (m) I gave him (some) durians today.

   (n) Tomorrow I shall get a letter from there.

   (o) We'd better write him a letter.

Fourth Week

A. Sentences

Satu (se-)	*One.*
Seorang India.	*One Indian.*
Seékor lembu.	*One cow.*
Seorang budak laki-laki.	*One boy.*
Dua orang budak laki-laki.	*Two boys.*
Tiga orang budak laki-laki.	*Three boys.*
Empat ékor lembu.	*Four cows.*
Lima ékor lembu.	*Five cows.*
Satu, dua, tiga, empat, lima.	*1, 2, 3, 4, 5.*
Dua orang Melayu dan tiga orang India.	*Two Malays and three Indians.*
Seorang Cina dan empat orang Melayu.	*One Chinese and four Malays.*
Tiga ékor anjing dan lima ékor kucing.	*Three dogs and five cats.*
Seékor lembu, seékor anjing dan seékor kucing.	*One cow, one dog and one cat.*

B. Word List

satu (se-)	*one*	dua	*two*
tiga	*three*	empat	*four*
lima	*five*	orang	*classifier for human beings*
ékor	*tail; cl. for animals*		
anjing	*dog*	kucing	*cat*

C. Grammar

(44) SATU

This form of the word is used only before a noun which does not have a classifier (see below), and when counting: one, two, three, etc. In other words *satu* is usually used only by itself. When it comes in front of another word, especially a classifier, it is shortened to *se* and is written as one word with it.

(45) SEORANG BUDAK LAKI-LAKI

Normally a numeral cannot come directly in front of a noun in Malay. A classifier, that is a word which tells what class of things we are talking about, must be inserted between the number and the noun enumerated. There are about forty of these classifiers, but fortunately we can manage very well with only four common ones, and we shall confine ourselves to these four for the moment. We shall learn one or two others later in the course, and a fuller list will be found in an appendix at the end of the book. Two of these four common classifiers refer to living creatures and two to inanimate objects. In this lesson we shall deal with the first two.

We use classifiers to a limited extent in English, too. We speak of twenty *head* of cattle, three *pints* of milk, etc., but most of our English ones are really expressions of quantity. The Malay ones, on the other hand, are more descriptive than quantitative.

Orang, which itself means *person,* is used to connect numbers to all words denoting persons. Strictly speaking, it should be used in front of itself, e.g. *dua orang-orang* but this sounds a bit odd, and so Malays prefer to say simply *dua orang,* two people. Examples:

seorang anak	*one child*
dua orang budak	*two youngsters*
tiga orang Melayu	*three Malays*
empat orang	*four people*

(46) SEEKOR LEMBU

Ékor basically means *tail*. Malays count animals by tails, not heads. This is possibly more logical, except perhaps in the case of a Manx cat or a guinea pig! Anyway, *ékor* is the classifier for all non-human living creatures of the animal kingdom. Examples:

seékor kucing	*one cat*
dua ékor lembu	*two cows*
lima ékor anjing	*five dogs*

Fourth Week   LESSON 17: TUESDAY

A. Sentences

Satu, dua, tiga, empat, lima.	*1, 2, 3, 4, 5.*
Enam, tujuh, lapan, sembilan, sepuluh.	*6, 7, 8, 9, 10.*
Sebuah buku.	*One book.*
Dua buah rumah.	*Two houses.*
Tiga buah keréta.	*Three cars.*
Empat buah kapal api.	*Four steamships.*
Lima buah kerétapi.	*Five railway trains.*
Enam biji rambutan.	*Six rambutans.*
Tujuh biji durian.	*Seven durians.*
Lapan biji limau.	*Eight limes.*
Sembilan biji manggis.	*Nine mangosteens.*
Sepuluh biji roti.	*Ten (bread) rolls.*
Berapa biji manggis encik mahu beli?	*How many mangosteens do you want to buy?*

Saya mahu beli sepuluh biji manggis.	*I want to buy ten mangosteens.*
Berapa ékor kucing ada di rumah encik?	*How many cats are there in your house?*
Di rumah saya ada tiga ékor kucing.	*In my house there are three cats.*
Encik ada berapa orang anak?	*How many children have you got?*
Saya ada seorang anak laki-laki dan seorang anak perempuan.	*I have one son and one daughter.*
Berapa buah rumah encik ada?	*How many houses have you got?*
Saya ada enam buah rumah.	*I've got six houses.*

B. Word List

enam	*six*	tujuh	*seven*
lapan	*eight*	sembilan	*nine*
sepuluh	*ten*	buah	*cl. for big things*
kapal api	*steamship*	biji	*seed; cl. for small*
roti	*bread*		*things*
berapa	*how much, how many*		

C. Grammar

(47) SEBUAH BUKU

   Buah, which we have already had meaning *fruit,* is used as a classifier for large objects, anything from a book to a battleship. Oddly enough, though, it is not used as a classifier for fruit; *biji* (seed) is used instead. *One fruit* is *se-biji buah.* See (48) below. Examples:

sebuah buku Melayu	*one Malay book*
dua buah kereta	*two cars*
tujuh buah kapal api.	*seven steamships*

(48) SEBIJI BUAH RAMBUTAN

Biji (seed) is the classifier for small objects like rambutans. golf balls, and so on. It is also the classifier for the word *buah* when it means *fruit*. Examples:

sebiji durian	*one durian*
sebiji bola golf	*one golf ball*

(49) LAPAN

Lapan is the colloquial form of *delapan*, which is dropping out of use even in writing nowadays.

(50) BERAPA

Berapa (how much, how many) is treated as a numeral and requires a classifier. Examples:

berapa orang budak laki-laki?	*how many boys?*
berapa ekor anjing?	*how many dogs?*
berapa buah kapal?	*how many ships?*
berapa biji roti?*	*how many rolls?*

Fourth Week   LESSON 18: WEDNESDAY

A. Sentences

Semalam saya naik keréta pergi ke pasar.	*Yesterday I went to the market by car.*
Apa encik mahu beli di pasar?	*What did you want to buy in the market?*
Saya mahu beli daging dan buah rambutan.	*I wanted to buy meat and some rambutans.*
Berapa biji rambutan encik beli?	*How many rambutans did you buy?*

* sebiji roti "a roll"
  sebantal roti "a loaf of bread."

Sepuluh biji.	*Ten.*
Berapa buah kedai makan ada di pasar?	*How many restaurants are there in the market?*
Ada tiga buah kedai makan di sana.	*There are three restaurants there.*
Sebuah kedai makan Melayu, sebuah kedai makan Cina, dan sebuah kedai makan India.	*One Malay restaurant, one Chinese restaurant, and one Indian restaurant.*
Encik makan di kedai makan Cina?	*Did you eat in the Chinese restaurant?*
Ya. Makan.	*Yes, I did.*
Berapa orang Cina ada di kedai makan itu semalam?	*How many Chinese were there in that restaurant yesterday?*
Ada sembilan orang Cina makan nasi, dan tujuh orang Cina makan daging babi.	*There were nine Chinese eating rice, and seven Chinese eating pork.*
Sebelas, dua belas, tiga belas.	*Eleven, twelve, thirteen.*
Empat belas, lima belas.	*Fourteen, fifteen.*
Enam belas, tujuh belas.	*Sixteen, seventeen.*
Lapan belas, sembilan belas.	*Eighteen, nineteen.*
Dua puluh.	*Twenty.*
Dua belas buah keréta dan sembilan belas buah keréta lembu.	*12 cars and 19 bullock carts.*
Dua puluh ékor lembu dan tiga belas ékor anjing.	*20 cows and 13 dogs.*
Sembilan belas biji durian dan enam belas biji manggis.	*19 durians and 16 mangosteens.*

| Dua belas orang India dan empat belas orang putih. | *12 Indians and 14 Europeans.* |

B. *Word List*

sebelas	*eleven*	dua belas	*twelve*
tiga belas	*thirteen*	empat belas	*fourteen*
lima belas	*fifteen*	enam belas	*sixteen*
tujuh belas	*seventeen*	lapan belas	*eighteen*
sembilan belas	*nineteen*	dua puluh	*twenty*

C. *Grammar*

(51) BELAS

Notice that the teens are formed simply by adding *belas* to the units. *Satu* as usual takes its shorter form, *se*.

(52) Revise the grammar of Lesson 16 and Lesson 17.

Fourth Week   LESSON 19: THURSDAY

A. *Sentences*

Sepuluh, dua puluh, tiga puluh.	*Ten, twenty, thirty.*
Empat puluh, lima puluh, enam puluh.	*Forty, fifty, sixty.*
Tujuh puluh, lapan puluh.	*Seventy, eighty.*
Sembilan puluh, seratus.	*Ninety, one hundred.*
Dua puluh, dua puluh satu, dua puluh dua.	*Twenty, twenty-one, twenty-two.*
Dua puluh tiga, dua puluh empat.	*Twenty-three, twenty-four.*
Dua puluh lima, dua puluh enam.	*Twenty-five, twenty-six.*

Dua puluh tujuh, dua puluh lapan.	*Twenty-seven, twenty-eight.*
Dua puluh sembilan, tiga puluh.	*Twenty-nine, thirty.*

Sembilan puluh sembilan buah keréta lembu.	*99 bullock carts.*
Tujuh puluh enam biji rambutan.	*76 rambutans.*
Lima puluh tiga orang Melayu.	*53 Malays.*
Seratus lapan puluh empat orang Cina.	*184 Chinese.*
Seratus tiga puluh sembilan ékor lembu.	*139 head of cattle.*
Di hospital itu ada seratus dua puluh orang sakit.	*In that hospital there are 120 patients.*
Ada seratus lima puluh lima orang penumpang naik kerétapi ini.	*There are 155 passengers travelling on this train.*
Ada lapan puluh tiga orang penumpang Melayu, dua belas orang penumpang India dan enam puluh orang penumpang Cina.	*There are 83 Malay passengers, 12 Indian passengers, and 60 Chinese passengers.*
Di kedai kopi itu ada lima belas orang Melayu dan enam orang Cina minum kopi.	*In that coffee-shop there are 15 Malays and 6 Chinese drinking coffee.*
Apa encik beli di pasar hari ini?	*What did you buy in the market today?*

Saya beli dua puluh biji rambutan dan tiga ékor ikan.	*I bought 20 rambutans and 3 fish.*
Encik beli telur?	*Did you buy any eggs?*
Ya. Saya beli dua belas biji telur.	*Yes, I did. I bought 12 eggs.*
Apa lagi encik beli di pasar?	*What else did you buy in the market?*
Apa lagi? Saya beli roti dan daging kambing.	*What else? I bought some bread and some mutton.*

B. Word List

tiga puluh	*thirty*	empat puluh	*forty*
lima puluh	*fifty*	enam puluh	*sixty*
tujuh puluh	*seventy*	lapan puluh	*eighty*
sembilan puluh	*ninety*	seratus	*one hundred*
ratus	*hundred*	penumpang	*passenger*
telur	*egg*	lagi	*else, more, still, yet*

C. Grammar

(53) TIGA PULUH

The tens are formed by adding *puluh* to the units. Again *satu* takes its shorter form *se*.

(54) DUA PULUH SATU

Above twenty the numbers are formed as in English by simple juxtaposition. The examples in Section A of this lesson will make this clearer than a long explanation.

Fourth Week LESSON 20: FRIDAY

A. Sentences

Seorang Melayu dan seorang India.	*One Malay and one Indian.*
Seékor kucing dan seékor anjing	*One cat and one dog.*
Sebantal roti dan sebiji rambutan.	*One loaf of bread and one rambutan.*
Sebuah kapal dan sebuah kerétapi.	*One ship and one train.*
Sebelas biji rambutan dan dua belas biji durian.	*11 rambutans and 12 durians.*
Tiga belas buah kapalapi dan empat belas buah keréta.	*13 steamships and 14 cars.*
Di Alor Setar ada lima buah panggung wayang gambar.	*In Alor Star there are five cinemas.*
Di kedai makan ini ada ramai orang makan nasi.	*In this restaurant there are a lot of people eating.*
Berapa orang ada?	*How many are there?*
Ada sebelas orang Cina, tujuh orang Melayu dan empat belas orang India.	*There are 11 Chinese, 7 Malays, and 14 Indians.*

B. Word List

No new words in this Lesson.

C. Grammar

(55) Revise the grammar of Lessons 16–19.

Fourth Week   REVISION LESSON D: WEEK-END

A. Sentences

Revise all the sentences in Lessons 16–20.

B. Word List

Revise all the word lists in Lessons 16–20.

C. Grammar

Revise all the grammar sections (44–54) in Lessons 16–19.

D. Exercises

(1) Make up twenty sentences using the material you have so far learnt. Keep to the sentence patterns in the course; it is unwise to try to invent your own at this stage.

(2) Read aloud the following conversation:

A. Encik pergi ke mana semalam?
B. Saya pergi ke Kuala Lumpur.

A. Apa encik buat di Kuala Lumpur?
B. Saya pergi ke sebuah kedai makan Cina.

A. Apa encik makan di kedai makan itu?
B. Saya makan nasi, daging babi dan tiga biji rambutan.

A. Ada ramai orang di kedai itu semalam?
B. Ada. Ada empat belas orang Cina makan nasi di sana; dan lagi ada dua tiga orang putih minum kopi. Orang Melayu dan orang India tak ada semalam.

A. Encik balik hari ini?

B. Ya. Saya naik kerétapi balik ke sini.
A. Encik tidak naik keréta balik ke sini?
B. Tidak. Saya tak ada keréta. Keréta saya, saya jual semalam di Kuala Lumpur.

(3) Translate the conversation in (2) into English.
(4) Insert the correct classifiers in the blanks:
   (a) Saya ada tiga _____ keréta.
   (b) Di kedai itu ada lima _____ Melayu.
   (c) Ada empat _____ penumpang naik keréta itu.
   (d) Berapa _____ durian encik beli di pasar?
   (e) Berapa _____ kucing ada di rumah encik?
(5) Read aloud (in Malay):
   3, 7, 9, 11, 14, 17, 18, 23, 26, 33, 44, 55, 57, 68, 77, 79, 80, 84, 86, 90, 93, 95, 99, 100, 106, 133, 154, 167, 178, 188, 190, 199
(6) Translate into Malay:
   (a) How many children have you got?
   (b) I've got two sons and three daughters.
   (c) My father has two cars.
   (d) I ate seven mangosteens yesterday.
   (e) That Malay has thirty head of cattle.
   (f) There are fifty-three passengers travelling on that train.
   (g) That steamship has a hundred passengers.
   (h) My mother bought twenty-four eggs in the Malay market.
   (i) My daughter likes eating eggs.
   (j) In this hospital there are 150 patients.

A. Sentences

Buah durian ini berapa
harganya?

How much are these durians?

Buah durian ini harganya
tujuh puluh sén
sebiji.

*These durians are seventy
cents each.*

Buku ini berapa harganya?

How much is this book?

Buku ini harganya dua
ringgit lima puluh sén.

This book is $2.50.

Encik ada berapa banyak
wang?

*How much money have you
got?*

Saya ada seringgit
tiga puluh tiga
sén sahaja.

I've got only $1.33.

Sepuluh sén.

Ten cents (South Malaya).

Sekupang.

Ten cents (North Malaya, esp.
Kedah and Penang.)

Dua kupang

Twenty cents (North Malaya).

Buah durian itu berapa
harganya?

*How much are those
durians?*

Durian itu harganya enam
kupang sebiji.

*Those durians are sixty cents
each* (North).

Dan buah durian besar
ini berapa harganya?

*And how much are these
big durians?*

Buah durian besar ini
lapan kupang lima duit
sebiji.

*These big durians are eighty-
five cents each.*

Daging lembu itu berapa
harganya sekati?

*How much is that beef a
catty?*

Daging lembu ini dua
ringgit sekupang sekati.

This beef is $2.10 a catty
(North).

Baiklah! Bagi saya tiga
kati.

*All right. Give me three
catties.*

Berapa harganya itu?	*How much is that?*
Tiga kati daging lembu ini harganya enam ringgit tiga kupang.	*Three catties of this beef cost $6.30.*
Daging kambing tak ada hari ini?	*Haven't you got any mutton today?*
Hari ini tak ada. Semalam ada.	*Not today. I had some yesterday.*
Daging kambing itu semalam berapa harganya?	*How much was the mutton yesterday?*
Dua ringgit tiga kupang sekati.	*$2.30 a catty.*

B. *Word List*

harga	*price*	nya	*its, his, her*
harganya	*cost*	sén	*cent*
ringgit	*dollar*	sahaja	*only*
kupang	*ten cents*	besar	*big, large, great*
kati	*catty* *	duit	*money, cent*
		wang	*money*

C. *Grammar*

(56) NYA

This is a "softened" form of *dia,* and may be used instead of *dia* except when *dia* is the subject. Examples:

bukunya	*his book*
téngoknya	*look at him*

NYA is written together as one word with the word to which it is added. *Harganya* is a set expression meaning literally *its price* but corresponding almost to the English *verb* "cost".

(57) SAHAJA

Usually pronounced *saja.*

* 3 catties = 4 pounds

(58) SEKUPANG

Unless the student is living in North Malaya, especially in the states of Penang and Kedah, he had better avoid the use of this word, which is just not understood by the majority of southerners. Nevertheless do not forget the word, because you will hear nothing else in the North, and you will need to know how to use it if you are travelling or doing business in Penang or Kedah. For that reason it is included in the lessons from time to time to remind you of its existence.

Fifth Week   LESSON 22: TUESDAY

A. Sentences

Encik pergi ke mana?	*Where are you going?*
Saya pergi ke pasar; saya mahu beli barang.	*I'm going to the market; I want to do some shopping.*
Apa encik mahu beli di pasar?	*What do you want to buy in the market?*
Saya mahu beli daging lembu dan buah manggis.	*I want to buy some beef and some mangosteens.*
Baik kita pergi ke kedai daging itu beli daging lembu.	*We'd better go to the butcher's shop and buy the beef.*
Baiklah. Daging lembu ada hari ini?	*Yes, all right. Have you any beef today?*
Ada. Ada banyak daging lembu di pasar hari ini.	*Yes, we have. There's a lot of beef in the market today.*
Daging lembu encik berapa harganya hari ini?	*How much is your beef today?*

Seringgit lapan puluh sén sekati. Sangat murah.

$1.80 a catty. It's very cheap.

Murah! Saya ingat seringgit lapan kupang mahal sangat.

Cheap! I think $1.80 is too dear.

Bukan mahal; murah. Daging saya daging nombor satu.

It's not dear; it's cheap. My meat is the very best quality.

Baiklah. Beri saya dua kati.

All right, then. Give me two catties.

Berapa harganya dua kati?

How much is two catties?

Tiga ringgit enam puluh sén.

$3.60.

Sekarang baik kita pergi ke pasar buah-buahan beli buah manggis.

Now we'd better go to the fruit market and buy the mangosteens.

Encik ada buah manggis?

Have you got any mangosteens?

Ada. Buah manggis harganya tiga puluh sén sepuluh biji.

Yes, I have. They are thirty cents for ten.

Buah manggis ini sangat baik; beri saya dua-puluh biji.

These mangosteens are very good; give me twenty of them.

Baiklah, encik. Dua puluh biji harganya enam puluh sén.

All right, sir. Twenty will cost sixty cents.

Encik mahu beli buah durian?

Do you want any durians?

Tidak. Hari ini saya tak mahu buah durian.

No, I don't want any durians today.

B. Word List

barang	*things, goods, luggage*	beli barang	*go shopping*
		murah	*cheap*
kedai daging	*butcher's shop*	mahal	*dear, expensive*
sangat	*very, very much*	nombor	*number*
nombor satu	*first class, best quality*	sekarang	*now*
		pasar buah-	
buah-buahan	*(all kinds of) fruit*	buahan	*fruit market*

C. Grammar

(59) MURAH SANGAT/SANGAT MURAH

In front of an adjective *sangat* means "very"; *after* an adjective it usually means "too", e.g.

sangat murah	*very cheap*
murah sangat	*too cheap*
sangat mahal	*very dear*
mahal sangat	*too dear*

When used with a verb, in the meaning of *very much*, *sangat* usually goes before the verb. Example:

saya sangat suka makan daging lembu.
I'm very fond of beef.

(60) BUKAN MAHAL; MURAH

An adjective is normally negated by *tidak*, e.g. *daging ini tidak mahal;* but when the adjective negated is immediately "corrected" by another adjective (as here), we must use *bukan* in place of *tidak*.

(61) PASAR BUAH-BUAHAN

Reduplication is common in Malay, and has various functions. We shall comment on each example as it occurs. In this case the reduplication, as often, indicates "all different kinds of", and is appropriate here because in a fruit market we do not expect to find only one kind of fruit.

Sometimes, as here, a reduplicated word takes in addition the suffix *an* with no change in meaning. It is not possible to predict which words do this and which do not: each case must be learnt as it occurs.

Fifth Week

A. Sentences

Saya hendak beli buah manggis.	*I'm going to buy some mangosteens.*
Bésok saya hendak pergi ke pasar.	*Tomorrow I'm going to go to the market.*
Orang itu hendak baca buku saya.	*That man is going to read my book.*
Saya hendak tulis surat kepada anak saya di Alor Setar.	*I'm going to write a letter to my ·son in Alor Star.*
Bésok saya nak pergi ke pasar.	*Tomorrow I'm going to go to the market.*
Orang itu nak baca buku saya.	*That man is going to read my book.*
Saya nak tulis surat kepada anak saya di Alor Setar.	*I'm going to write a letter to my son in Alor Star.*
Saya nak baca buku itu.	*I'm going to read that book.*
Saya mahu baca buku itu.	*I want to read that book.*
Saya nak beli keréta baharu.	*I'm going to buy a new car.*

Saya mahu beli
 keréta baharu.

I want to buy a new car.

Bésok saya nak beli
 daging babi di
 pasar Cina.

*Tomorrow I shall buy
 some pork in the
 Chinese market.*

Bésok saya mahu beli
 daging babi di
 pasar Cina.

*Tomorrow I shall want to
 buy some pork in the
 Chinese market.*

Encik nak ke mana?
Nak ke mana?
Saya nak ke hospital.
Kawan saya sakit.
 Saya ingat dia
 nak mati.*

Where are you off to?
Where are you off to?
I'm off to the hospital.
*My friend is ill. I think
 he's going to die.*

Semalam saya nak pergi
 téngok dia, tetapi
 ada banyak kerja,
 tak dapat pergi.

*Yesterday I was going to
 see him, but I had a
 lot of work, and so
 I didn't manage to go.*

Tetapi hari ini isteri
 dia kata kepada saya
 dia nak mati.*

*But today his wife told
 me that he was going
 to die.*

---

*These sentences might seem rather harsh to Malays, who do not like
referring directly to death and to whom the word *mati* is rather
shocking. A Malay would be more likely to say, *Kawan saya sakit; saya
ingat dia sakit kuat* [i.e. seriously ill]. The last sentence would probably
be rephrased by a Malay as follows: *Tetapi hari ini isteri dia kata kepada
saya, dia sakit kuat.* The normal meaning of *kuat* is "strong", but the
phrase *sakit kuat* corresponds to the English "seriously ill".

B. Word List

hendak (nak)	*going to,*	kawan	*friend*
(nak)	*intend to,*	ingat	*think, remember*
	will, shall	mati	*die, be dead*
tetapi	*but*	kerja	*work* (n.)
isteri	*wife*	kata	*say*
kata kepada	*tell, inform*	nak ke	*to be off to*
baharu	*new*		

C. Grammar

(62) SAYA HENDAK BELI BUAH MANGGIS

Hendak in front of another verb indicates the intention of performing whatever action is denoted by the verb in question. It gives the following verb an almost future meaning, and is in fact the nearest equivalent in spoken Malay to the English future tense. Its meaning corresponds very closely to the English *to be going to.*

In colloquial speech *hendak* is almost always pronounced *nak,* and indeed is often so written.

(63) HENDAK and MAHU

These two words must not be confused. *Mahu* means *want* and is never used in the future-sense of *hendak.*

(64) NAK KE MANA?

In this very common idiom the verb *pergi* is omitted, as it often is when the preposition *ke* is present. *Nak* followed by *ke* is more or less equivalent to the English *off to.*

(65) TETAPI

Colloquially usually pronounced *tapi.*

Fifth Week

A. Sentences

Bapa encik nak ke
mana semalam?

*Where was your father off
to yesterday?*

Dia naik keréta nak
pergi ke Kuala
Lumpur.

*He was off to Kuala Lumpur
by car.*

Dia nak buat apa
di sana?

*What is he going to do
there?*

Dia nak jual keréta
dia kepada seorang
kawan dia.

*He's going to sell his car
to one of his friends.*

Macam mana dia nak
balik ke sini?

*How's he going to get
back here?*

Dia nak beli sebuah
keréta baharu di
Kuala Lumpur.

*He's going to buy a new
car in Kuala Lumpur.*

Encik nak ke mana
sekarang?

Where are you off to now?

Saya nak ke pasar
beli barang.

*I'm off to the market to
buy some things.*

Barang apa encik nak
beli?

*What things are you going
to buy?*

Saya nak pergi ke
sebuah kedai buku, nak
beli kalam, dakwat
dan kertas tulis.

*I'm going to a bookshop to
buy a pen, some ink
and some writing paper.*

Apa encik nak buat
dengan barang itu?

*What are you going to do
with those things?*

Saya nak tulis surat
kepada bapa saya di
Kota Baharu.

*I'm going to write a letter
to my father in Kota
Bahru.*

Lepas itu, apa encik
nak buat?

*After that, what are you
going to do?*

Lepas itu saya nak makan nasi.	*After that I'm going to eat.*
Encik nak makan di rumah?	*Are you going to eat at home?*
Tidak. Saya nak makan di sebuah kedai makan Melayu.	*No. I'm going to eat in a Malay restaurant.*
Di mana kedai makan itu?	*Where is it?*
Kedai makan itu ada di pekan; encik mahu pergi sama?	*It's in the town; do you want to come too?*
Mahulah. Saya sangat suka makan makanan Melayu.	*Rather! I am very fond of Malay food.*
Apa kita boléh makan di kedai makan itu?	*What can we eat in that restaurant?*
Kita boléh makan nasi dengan gulai.	*We can eat rice and curry.*
Baguslah. Saya sangat suka makan gulai Melayu.	*Splendid! I am very fond of Malay curry.*
Tetapi gulai di kedai makan itu sangat pedas.	*But the curry in that restaurant is very hot.*
Tak apa. Saya sangat suka makan makanan pedas.	*It doesn't matter. I am very fond of hot food.*

B. Word List

macam	*kind, sort; like, as, as if*	mana macam	*which*
kedai buku	*bookshop*	mana	*how*
		kalam	*pen*
kertas	*paper*	dakwat	*ink*

dengan	*with*	kertas tulis	*writing paper*
lepas itu	*after that,*	lepas	*after, beyond*
	afterwards	pekan	*town*
sama	*together (with),*	pergi sama	*to go too*
	along (with),	datang	*to come*
	same, too	sama	*too*
makanan	*food*	gulai	*curry*
bagus	*splendid, fine,*	pedas	*(pepper) hot*
	beautiful,	tak apa	*it doesn't matter,*
	excellent		*not to worry.*

C. Grammar

(66) SEORANG KAWAN DIA

Note the Malay construction. Translate: *one of his friends,* or *a friend of his.*

(67) Note that Malay has three words for "rice", which must be carefully distinguished from each other:

padi	*[growing] rice*
beras	*[uncooked but harvested] rice*
nasi	*[cooked] rice*

One therefore *grows padi, buys and sells beras,* and *eats nasi.*

(68) DI RUMAH

Literally, *in the house,* this is the usual expression for *at home.*

(69) ENCIK MAHU PERGI SAMA?

Notice the Malay idiom. Malays use *pergi* (and not *datang*) here because the two men have not yet started out. When they arrive at their destination one of them will be able to say to the other, *encik datang sama, you came too.*

(70) PEDAS

There are three words you will have to know in Malay to render the one English word *hot*, viz.:

pedas	*hot, of curry, pepper, etc.*
hangat	*hot, in most other ways (this is the most usual word for* hot*)*
panas	*hot, of something that has been standing in the direct rays of the sun.*

Examples:

Makanan ini ada banyak lada; sangat pedas.

There's a lot of pepper in this food; it's very hot.

Gulai Sri Lanka sangat pedas.

Sri Lanka curry is very hot.

Air ini hangat.

This water is hot (because it has been boiled, etc.).

Air ini panas.

This water is hot (because it has been standing in the sun).

Panas hari ini.

It's a hot day today (because the sun is beating mercilessly down, etc.).

Hangat hari ini.

It's a hot day today (this implies that it is hot weather even though the sun is hidden behind dense clouds).

(71) TAK APA

One of the commonest expressions in everyday spoken Malay. Literally meaning *not anything*, it has come to have the same force as the French *ca ne fait rien*. In English it may be translated in a dozen different ways according to the context, e.g. it doesn't matter, don't bother, I couldn't care less, not to worry, etc., etc.

Short for *tidak apa*, its corrupted bazaar form *tidapa* has given rise to the "English" word *tidapathy*, a word very expressive of the attitude of *couldn't-care-less-ness* that grips all of us from time to time!

Fifth Week

A. Sentences

Cik Zainal nak ke mana?	*Where are you going, Zainal?*
Saya nak ke pasar.	*I'm off to the market.*
Saya boléh pergi sama?	*Can I come too?*
Boléhlah. Apa Encik Mat nak beli?	*Of course you can. What do you want to buy, Mat?*
Saya nak beli pén baharu di sebuah kedai buku.	*I am going to buy a new pen in a bockshop.*
Baiklah, mari kita pergi.	*All right; come on, let's go.*
Kedai ini kedai buku; boléh beli pén di sini.	*This shop's a bookshop; you can buy pens here.*
Pén ini berapa harganya?	*How much is this pen?*
Pén ini nombor satu; harganya dua belas ringgit.	*This pen's a very good one; it costs $12.00.*
Itu mahal sangat. Pén murah tak ada?	*That's too dear. Haven't you got any cheap pens?*
Ada.	*Yes, I have.*
Berapa harganya pén ini?	*How much is this pen?*
Pén ini sangat murah; harganya dua ringgit sebatang.	*These pens are very cheap; they are two dollars each.*
Baiklah; saya nak beli sebatang sahaja.	*All right; I'll just buy one.*

B. Word List

Cik	*Mrs, Miss*	batang	cl. *for stick-like objects*
Encik	*Mr.*		

C. Grammar

(72) ENCIK ZAINAL

Encik as a title is used only before the names of men and *Cik* is used before the names of men and women. It therefore corresponds to the English courtesy titles *Mr, Mrs,* and *Miss.* The only difference is that Malays use this courtesy title more frequently than we do in English. Friends quite commonly address each other with it, where we in English would use Christian names, especially when a younger person is talking to an older, or an inferior to a superior. A wife uses it to her husband, and a younger brother to an elder brother, for example.

(73) SEBATANG KALAM

Here we have another classifier. *Batang* is used as a classifier for stick-shaped objects, e.g. pens, pencils, walking-sticks, cigars, cigarettes, etc.

Fifth Week   REVISION LESSON E: WEEK-END

A. Sentences

Revise all the sentences in Lessons 21–25.

B. Word List

Revise all the word lists in Lessons 21–25.

C. Grammar

Revise all the grammar sections (56–73) in Lessons 21–25.

D. Exercises

(1) Make up twenty sentences using what you have already learnt.

(2) Read aloud the following conversation:

A. Apa khabar, encik?

B. Khabar baik. Encik nak ke mana?

A. Saya nak pergi ke pasar beli barang. Lepas itu saya nak pergi ke sebuah kedai makan, makan nasi.

B. Saya boléh pergi sama?

A. Boléhlah.

B. Apa encik nak beli di pasar?

A. Saya nak beli ikan, daging dan buah durian.

B. Tetapi hari ini ikan sangat mahal; baik encik beli daging sahaja.

A. Saya tak tahu ikan sangat mahal; isteri saya kata ikan murah di pekan ini.

B. Tidak! Ikan di sini sangat mahal.

A. Baiklah! Saya tidak nak beli. Di mana ada sebuah kedai makan Melayu? Saya sangat suka makan gulai Melayu.

B. Di pasar Melayu ada dua buah kedai makan baik. Kita boléh pergi ke kedai makan itu di sana. Gulai kedai itu nombor satu. Saya nak pergi sama makan di sana. Boléh?

A. Boléhlah! Mari kita pergi makan sekarang. Lepas itu kita boleh beli barang untuk* isteri saya.

B. Encik suka makan gulai pedas? Di kedai itu gulai sangat pedas.

A. Sukalah. Lagi pedas lagi baik.**

B. Apa kita nak minum dengan gulai?

A. Baik kita minum air sahaja.

---

untuk: "for; in order to."

** Notice this idiom: *lagi....lagi....*, "The more....The more...."

(3) Translate the conversation in (2) into English.
(4) Read off the following prices in Malay, (i) in the southern way and (ii) in the northern way:

$3.50; $10.25; $0.60; $56.70; $136.45

(5) Translate into Malay:

(a) I'm going to the market to do some shopping; afterwards I'm going to have a meal in a Chinese restaurant. Do you want to come too?

(b) Rather! I'm very fond of Chinese food. Is the food good in that restaurant?

(c) Where did you buy that new car? I bought it in Singapore yesterday. Do you want to ride (in it)?

(d) Yesterday I got a letter from my mother in Seremban. She says that my father is in hospital in Kuala Lumpur.

(e) How much is this book? It costs $15.00. That's very dear. No, it isn't dear; it's cheap. This book is very good.

(f) That European is very fond of very hot Malay curry. He says, "The hotter, the better."

(g) I didn't know Europeans ate curry. Oh yes, they do. Many Europeans are very fond of Malay food.

(h) Where are you going tomorrow? I'm going to Kuala Kangsar to see my sick father. My mother thinks he is seriously ill.

(i) This tea is very hot; I can't drink (it).

(j) This curry is very hot; he can't eat (it).

A. Sentences

Hari ini hari apa?	*What day is it today?*
Hari ini hari Senin.	*Today is Monday.*
Hari apa semalam?	*What day was it yesterday?*
Semalam hari Ahad.	*Yesterday was Sunday.*
Esok hari apa?	*What day will it be tomorrow?*
Esok hari Selasa.	*Tomorrow will be Tuesday.*
Hari Ahad, hari Senin, hari Selasa.	*Sunday, Monday, Tuesday.*

Berapa hari ada dalam satu minggu?	*How many days are there in one week?*
Dalam satu minggu ada tujuh hari.	*In a week there are seven days.*
Encik pergi ke mana hari Ahad?	*Where did you go on Sunday?*
Pada hari Ahad saya pergi ke pekan nak téngok wayang gambar.	*On Sunday I went to the pictures in town.*
Apa encik nak buat hari ini?	*What are you going to do today?*
Hari ini hari Senin; pada hari Senin saya selalu pergi ke pejabat.	*Today is Monday; on Monday I always go to the office.*
Bésok hari Selasa; apa encik nak buat bésok?	*Tomorrow is Tuesday; what are you going to do tomorrow?*
Bésok saya nak pergi ke rumah seorang kawan saya nak makan malam.	*Tomorrow I am going to the house of a friend of mine for dinner.*
Lusa encik boléh datang ke rumah	*The day after tomorrow can you come to my*

saya makan malam? *house for dinner?*

Boléhlah! Terima kasih, encik. *Certainly. Thank you very much.*

Sama-sama. *Not at all.*

Berapa hari ada dalam satu bulan? *How many days are there in one month?*

Ada lebih kurang tiga puluh hari dalam satu bulan. *There are approximately thirty days in one month.*

B. Word List

hari Senin	*Monday*	hari Ahad	*Sunday*
hari Selasa	*Tuesday*	dalam	*in, inside*
minggu	*week*	selalu	*always, usually*
pejabat	*office*	sama-	*same to you; not*
lebih	*more, in excess*	sama	*at all; don't*
lebih kurang	*approximately, more or less*		*mention it*
		kurang	*less, minus*
lusa	*the day after tomorrow*	bulan	*month; moon*
		ésok	*tomorrow*
pada	*on, at*		

C. Grammar

(74) SENIN, AHAD, SELASA

These are really Malay forms of Arabic words. *Ahad* is from the Arabic *ahad* "one", *senin* is from *ithnain* "two" and *selasa* comes from the Arabic *thalatha* "three," so that Sunday, Monday and Tuesday are really *first, second,* and *third day* respectively.

(75) BÉSOK, ÉSOK

These are simply alternative forms of the same word. There is no difference in meaning.

(76) SATU MINGGU, SATU BULAN

Words like *hari, minggu,* and *bulan* are really expressions of quantity (of time) and therefore do not need a classifier. They are in fact almost classifiers themselves. As a result it is perfectly all right to use the full form of *satu* before them, although the shortened form *se-* is also permissible. In this case *satu* is stronger than *se*, i.e.:

satu hari	*one day*
sehari	*a day*
satu minggu	*one week*
seminggu	*a week*
satu bulan	*one month*
sebulan	*a month*

(77) (PADA) HARI AHAD

The preposition *pada* is the correct one for *on* or *at* when these two English prepositions precede expressions of time. *Pada* may, however, be omitted in speaking, although it should be retained in written Malay.

(78) SAYA PERGI KE PEKAN NAK TENGOK WAYANG GAM-BAR

Notice the use of *nak* here. It is almost equivalent to the English *to* when *to* means *in order to*, i.e. with the intention of. *Nak* is very commonly used in such a context. It may be omitted, but the sentence sounds better with it in. Similar uses of *nak* will be discussed as we come to them. Here it expresses purpose or intention.

(79) SAMA-SAMA

This is the stock answer to *terima kasih*.

Sixth Week.

A. Sentences

Kelmarin dahulu hari Ahad.	*The day before yesterday was Sunday.*
Semalam hari Senin	*Yesterday was Monday.*
Hari ini hari Selasa.	*Today is Tuesday.*
Bésok hari Rabu.	*Tomorrow will be Wednesday.*
Lusa hari Khamis.	*The day after tomorrow will be Thursday.*
Hari Ahad, hari Senin, hari Selasa, hari Rabu, hari Khamis.	*Sunday, Monday, Tuesday, Wednesday, Thursday.*
Hari apa encik bercuti?	*What day do you have off?*
Saya selalu bercuti pada hari Ahad.	*I always have Sunday off.*
Tiap-tiap hari Ahad saya suka pergi ke Batu Feringgi.	*Every Sunday I like to go to Batu Feringgi.*
Di mana Batu Feringgi itu?*	*Where is Batu Feringgi?*
Di Pulau Pinang.	*It's in Penang.*
Apa encik buat tiap-tiap hari Ahad di Batu Feringgi?	*What do you do every Sunday at Batu Feringgi?*
Saya pergi ke sana nak duduk di pantai.	*I go there and sit on the beach.*

---

* *itu* here is used to mean "that one that you mentioned just now", "that place you called Batu Feringgi", or "that well-known Batu Feringgi". Cf. Latin: *ille Caesar*, "that well-known chap Caesar."

Boléh berenang di sana?	*Can one swim there?*
Boléh; tetapi ada banyak ular selimpat; berbahaya sikit nak berenang.	*Yes, one can; but there are a lot of sea-snakes; it's a bit dangerous to go swimming.*
Seribu.	*One thousand.*
Dua ribu, tiga ribu, empat ribu.	*2000, 3000, 4000.*
Lima ribu, enam ribu, tujuh ribu.	*5000, 6000, 7000.*
Lapan ribu, sembilan ribu.	*8000, 9000.*
Sepuluh ribu.	*10,000.*
Seribu sembilan ratus lima puluh tujuh.	*1957.*
Pada tahun seribu sembilan ratus lima puluh tujuh.	*In the year 1957.*

B. Word List

dahulu	*previously, before, earlier, ago*	kelmarin dahulu	*the day before yesterday*
hari Rabu	*Wednesday*	hari Khamis	*Thursday*
bercuti	*be on leave, go on leave*	tiap-tiap	*every, each*
		Pulau Pinang	*Penang (Island)*
pulau	*island*	(buah)	*areca nut, betel*
pantai	*beach, shore*	pinang	*nut*
berenang	*swim*	ular	*snake*
selimpat	*braided-ribbon pattern in lace*	ular selimpat	*sea-snake*
		berbahaya	*dangerous*
sikit	*a little, a bit, rather*	ribu	*thousand*
		seribu	*a thousand*
tahun	*year*		

C. Grammar

(80) DAHULU

Almost invariably pronounced, and sometimes written, *dulu*.

(81) HARI RABU, HARI KHAMIS

Rabu is a corruption of the Arabic *arbaa* (four) and *Khamis* is from the Arabic *Khamsa* (five).

(82) PULAU PINANG

Literally, Areca-Nut Island. This really refers to the whole island although it is often used without the *Pulau* to refer to the city of Georgetown. Locally, however, Georgetown is usually called *Tanjung* (point, headland), presumably because it is built on a point of land. People in Kedah, especially, always say *saya nak pi Tanjung* for *I'm going to Penang*.

(83) BERBAHAYA SIKIT

Sikit used after an adjective has the force of *rather, a bit*.

(84) BERBAHAYA SIKIT NAK BERENANG

"It's a bit dangerous to go swimming". Notice the construction: *nak* here has almost the meaning of the English *to* used before an infinitive. Indeed, in modern Malay it is coming to be used more and more like that, especially in writing in the form *hendak*. Perhaps, however, the original meaning of "intention" is not far away in this case, if we remember that Malay is an elliptical language and often leaves out words which would be necessary in English, leaving the meaning to be "filled out" from the context. The original meaning here is probably—*it's a bit dangerous (if you) intend to swim.*

Nevertheless, however we explain it, the fact remains that *hendak* in writing and *nak* in speaking frequently are used to join together two verbs or an adjective and a verb just like *to* in English. We should be on our guard against trying to be too profound in our analysis of another language; too often we run the risk of subconsciously putting our own thoughts into the minds of the people whose language we are studying. We must always deal with the facts as they are, and not try to interpret them in the light of some preconceived theory.

(85) RIBU

The formation of the thousands is just like that of the teens, tens and hundreds. Simply add *ribu* to the simple number.

(86) PADA TAHUN 1957

In English we have two ways of reading off such a group of figures. If 1957 is a number in arithmetic we usually read it, *one thousand nine hundred and fifty-seven,* but when it is the name of a year we say *nineteen hundred and fifty-seven* or *nineteen fifty-seven.* In Malay the second method is unknown; only the first method is used in both cases, except that when the number is the name of a year, the word *tahun* is almost always prefixed.

Sixth Week   LESSON 28: WEDNESDAY

A. Sentences

Hari ini hari Rabu.	*Today is Wednesday.*
Bésok hari Khamis.	*Tomorrow is Thursday.*
Lusa hari Jumaat.	*The day after tomorrow will be Friday.*
Hari Sabtu.	*Saturday.*
Hari Ahad, hari Senin, hari Selasa.	*Sunday, Monday, Tuesday.*

Hari Rabu, hari Khamis, hari Jumaat, hari Sabtu.	*Wednesday, Thursday, Friday, Saturday.*
Pada satu haribulan Januari.	*On the first of January.*
Pada tiga puluh satu haribulan Ogos tahun seribu sembilan ratus lima puluh tujuh Malaya dapat kemerdékaan.	*On the 31st of August 1957 Malaya gained her independence.*
Hari ini berapa haribulan?	*What's the date today?*
Hari ini dua puluh lima haribulan Septémber tahun se-ribu sembilan ratus lima puluh lapan.	*Today is the 25th of September 1958.*
Satu hari bulan Januari tahun baharu orang Inggeris.	*The 1st of January is the English New Year.*
Saya nak bercuti daripada enam hari-bulan Oktober sampai lima haribulan November.	*I shall be on leave from the 6th of October until the 5th of November.*
Pada tahun seribu sembilan ratus empat-puluh satu orang Jepun datang ke Malaya.	*In the year 1941 the Japanese came to Malaya.*
Pada tahun seribu sembilan ratus empat	*In the year 1945 the English came back*

puluh lima orang Inggeris balik ke Malaya.	*to Malaya.*
Pada tahun seribu lima ratus sebelas orang Portugis sampai ke Melaka.	*In the year 1511 the Portuguese arrived in Malacca.*
Pada tahun seribu tujuh ratus lapan puluh enam Yang Maha Mulia Sultan Kedah beri Pulau Pinang kepada orang Inggeris.	*In the year 1786 His Highness the Sultan of Kedah gave Penang Island to the English.*
Berapa bulan ada dalam satu tahun?	*How many months are there in one year?*
Dalam satu tahun ada dua belas bulan.	*In one year there are 12 months.*
Berapa hari ada dalam satu tahun?	*How many days are there in one year?*
Dalam satu tahun ada tiga ratus enam puluh lima hari.	*In one year there are 365 days.*

B. Word List

hari Jumaat	*Friday*	hari Sabtu	*Saturday*
kemerdékaan	*independence*	sampai	*arrive, reach; until*
Jepun	*Japanese* (adj).		
orang Jepun	*Japanese* (n.)	Portugis	*Portuguese* (adj.)
orang Portugis	*Portuguese* (n.)	Yang Maha Mulia	*His Highness*
Kedah	*Kedah*		
sultan	*sultan*		

C. *Grammar*

(87) HARI JUMAAT

Jumaat is from the Arabic *jama'ah* which means *assembly* or *gathering*. Friday is, of course the day when Muslims assemble or gather together at the mosque to pray. Hence *hari Jumaat* for *Friday*.

(88) HARI SABTU

Sabtu is from the Arabic *sabt* and is connected with the Hebrew *shabbath* both of which mean *idleness*. From this we get the English *sabbath*. Originally the Jews had their sabbath on Saturday (and indeed still have it then), the Christians changed it to Sunday, and were followed later by the Muslims, who fixed Friday as their day of rest. The old name *sabtu*, however, seems to have lost its real meaning by then, and so it has been retained to mean Saturday. Only the Jews, however, are really using it correctly.

(89) BULAN JANUARI

The Malay calendar is the Muslim one and is based on the moon rather than the sun. The Malay months, therefore, do not correspond at all with the European months. For this reason the Malays in their dealings with other races are courteous enough to use the Western calendar. They use the English[*] names of the months, usually preceded by the word *bulan*. For practical purposes there is no need for the non-Malay to learn the Malay names of the months of the Muslim calendar, although it would be considered a courtesy by the Malays if one did so. For this reason the Malay months have not been given in the body of this book, but will be found—for those interested enough to learn them—in the appendix on the Muslim calendar at the end of the book.

[*] The names are nowadays spelt in accordance with Malay phonetics, viz. Januari, Februari, Mac, April, Mei, Jun, Julai, Ogos, Septémber, Oktober, Novémber, Disémber.

(90) DATES

Study carefully the examples given of the Malay way of expressing dates. These examples will prove more useful than a long explanation.

(91) KEMERDÉKAAN

In colloquial language, and nowadays quite often in writing, this is usually substituted by the word *merdéka*. *Merdéka* is, strictly speaking, an adjective meaning *independent*, as may be seen from the phrase *Malaysia Merdéka* which means *Independent Malaysia* and not the *independence of Malaysia*. The student will be safer if he sticks to *kemerdékaan* for the noun and *merdéka* for the adjective. He will then be less likely to make grammatical errors in their use.

Sixth Week   LESSON 29: THURSDAY

A. Sentences

Hari ini hari apa?	*What day is it today?*
Hari ini hari Khamis.	*Today is Thursday.*
Hari ini berapa haribulan?	*What's the date today?*
Hari ini dua puluh enam haribulan Septémber.	*Today is the 26th of September.*
Pada hari Jumaat ramai orang Melayu sembahyang di mesjid.	*On Fridays a lot of Malays pray in the mosque.*
Di mana orang Inggeris sembahyang?	*Where do the English pray?*
Orang Inggeris sembahyang di geréja pada hari Ahad.	*English people pray in church on Sundays.*

Di mana orang Hindu (orang India) sembahyang?

Where do the Hindus (Indians) pray?

Orang India sembahyang di kuil Hindu.

Indians pray in Hindu temples.

Di mana orang Cina sembahyang?

Where do the Chinese pray?

Orang Cina sembahyang di tokong Cina.

The Chinese pray in a temple.

Minggu lepas saya pergi ke Kuala Lumpur.

Last week I went to Kuala Lumpur.

Minggu ini saya nak tinggal di Pulau Pinang.

This week I'm going to stay in Penang.

Minggu depan saya nak pergi bercuti ke Singapura.

Next week I'm going to to go to Singapore.

Tahun lepas saya bekerja di Raub.

Last year I was working in Raub.

Tahun ini saya bekerja di Kuantan.

This year I am working in Kuantan.

Tahun depan saya nak pergi ke England bercuti.

Next year I'm going to England on leave.

Daripada hari Senin sampai hari Jumaat saya bekerja di pejabat.

From Monday to Friday I work in the office.

Tetapi pada hari Sabtu dan hari Ahad saya bercuti.

But on Saturday and Sunday I have a holiday.

Pada hari Sabtu
 saya selalu pergi
 ke pantai nak
 berenang.

On Saturday I always go
 to the beach to
 swim.

Tetapi pada hari
 Ahad saya suka
 tinggal di rumah
 baca buku.

But on Sunday I like to
 stay at home and
 read a book.

B. Word List

sembahyang	*pray; prayer*	mesjid	*mosque*
geréja	*church*	kuil	*(Hindu) temple*
tokong	*(Chinese)*	Hindu	*Hindu (adj.)*
	temple	minggu	*last week*
orang Hindu	*Hindu (n)*	lepas	
tahun lepas	*last year*	minggu	*next week*
tahun	*next year*	depan	
depan		depan	*next; front*
bekerja	*work (vb.)*		

C. Grammar

(92) DARIPADA.....SAMPAI

   Notice that we use *daripada* and not *dari* with expressions of time.

Sixth Week   LESSON 30: FRIDAY

A. Sentences

Tujuh kosong enam lima.	*7065 (on the 'phone).*
Sejuta.	*One million.*
Sejuta, dua juta, tiga juta, empat juta, dll.	*One million, two million, three million, four million, etc.*
Tiga juta enam ratus lima puluh lapan ribu tujuh ratus tiga puluh empat.	*3,658,734.*
Satu tahun ada dua belas bulan.	*One year has twelve months.*
Satu bulan ada empat minggu.	*One month has four weeks.*
Satu minggu ada tujuh hari.	*One week has seven days.*
Satu hari ada dua puluh empat jam.	*One day has 24 hours.*
Satu jam ada enam puluh minit.	*One hour has 60 minutes.*
Satu minit ada enam puluh saat.	*One minute has 60 seconds.*

B. Word List

kosong	*empty; nought*	juta	*million*
sejuta	*one million*	jam	*hour; watch, clock*
minit	*minute*	saat	*second*

C. Grammar

(93) SEJUTA

One million. The millions are formed quite normally with the word *juta* as in the examples in Section A.

Sixth Week   REVISION LESSON F: WEEK-END

A. Sentences

Revise all the sentences in Lessons 26—30.

B. Word List

Revise all the word lists in Lessons 26—30.

C. Grammar

Revise all the grammar sections (74—93) in Lessons 26—30.

D. Exercises

(1) Make up thirty sentences using what you have so far learnt during the course.

(2) Read aloud the following conversation:

A. Apa khabar, encik?

B. Khabar baik, encik. Encik nak ke mana?

A. Saya nak ke pekan.

B. Apa encik nak buat di pekan?

A. Saya nak beli sebuah keréta baharu.

B. Tetapi encik ada sebuah keréta besar.

A. Keréta itu saya jual di Ipoh pada hari Sabtu lepas.

B. Berapa harga encik jual keréta itu?

A. Keréta itu saya jual tiga ribu lima ratus ringgit. Keréta itu sangat besar, saya nak beli keréta kecil.*

B. Berapa harga encik nak beli keréta baharu?

A. Saya ingat nak beli keréta harga empat-ribu lebih kurang.

B. Saya boléh pergi ke pekan dengan encik? Saya tahu di mana encik boléh beli sebuah keréta yang baik.**

*kecil: small, little.
**c.f. (160) P. 199

A. Boléhlah.; Terimakasih, encik.

B. Lepas itu encik nak buat apa di pekan?

A. Saya ingat nak makan di kedai makan Cina. Encik suka·makan makanan Cina?

B. Sukalah.

A. Baik encik pergi sama; boléh makan dengan saya.

B. Terima kasih, encik.

A. Sama-sama.

(3) Translate the conversation in (2) into English.

(4) Translate into Malay:

(a) Yesterday I sold my car in Kuala Lumpur; I got $4,500 (for it).

(b) Tomorrow I am going to buy a new car in Singapore.

(c) The day before yesterday was Saturday; I was on leave (for) two days; I went to Batu Feringgi in Penang to swim.

(d) A friend of mine said, "It's rather dangerous to swim at Batu Feringgi; there's a lot of sea-snakes there; you'd better just sit on the beach."

(e) Malays like eating areca nut, but Europeans don't like eating it.

(f) Kedah people do not say, "I am going to the Island of Penang"; they usually say, "I'm going (to) the Point."

(g) Many Malays do not like eating Chinese food; Chinese food has a lot of pork (in it). Malays cannot eat pork.

(h) The town of Alor Star has about 50,000 people.

(i) Malaya has approximately six million people.

(j) England has more or less fifty million people.

A. Sentences

Pukul satu.

One o'clock.

Pada pukul satu
saya selalu
makan nasi.

At one o'clock I always eat.

Pada pukul dua
saya balik ke-
pejabat.

At two o'clock I go back to the office.

Pada pukul tiga
saya selalu
minum secawan téh
di pejabat.

At three o'clock I always drink a cup of tea in the office.

Pada pukul empat
saya selalu pergi
ke Pejabat Pos.

At four o'clock I always go to the Post Office.

Pada pukul lima
saya selalu balik
ke rumah.

At five o'clock I always go home.

Pada pukul enam
saya selalu mandi.

At six o'clock I always have a bath.

Daripada pukul
tujuh sampai
pukul lapan saya
selalu baca suratkhabar.

From seven o'clock until eight o'clock I always read the newspaper.

Pada pukul sembilan
saya makan malam.

At nine o'clock I have dinner.

Daripada pukul se-
puluh sampai pukul
sebelas saya
baca buku.

From ten o'clock until eleven o'clock I read.

Pada pukul dua belas saya tidur.	*At twelve o'clock I go to bed.*
Pukul berapa encik bangun pagi?	*What time do you get up in the morning?*
Saya bangun pada pukul tujuh pagi.	*I get up at seven o'clock in the morning.*
Pada pukul berapa encik makan pagi?	*At what time do you have breakfast?*
Saya makan pagi pada pukul lapan.	*I have breakfast at eight o'clock.*
Pukul berapa encik pergi ke pejabat?	*What time do you go to the office?*
Saya selalu pergi ke pejabat pada pukul sembilan.	*I always go to the office at nine o'clock.*
Pukul berapa encik balik?	*What time do you come home?*
Saya selalu balik pada pukul satu.	*I always come home at one o'clock.*
Apa encik buat pada pukul se- puluh semalam?	*What were you doing at ten o'clock yesterday?*
Semalam pada pukul sepuluh pagi saya bekerja di pejabat.	*Yesterday at ten o'clock in the morning I was work- ing in the office.*

B. *Word List*

pelajaran	*lesson; education*	pukul	*strike; beat; o'clock*
cawan	*cup*	mandi	*have a bath; bathe, wash*
Pejabat Pos	*post office*		

tidur	sleep; go to sleep;	bangun	get up, rise
	go to bed	makan	have breakfast;
pagi	morning, in the	pagi	breakfast
	morning		

C. Grammar

(93a) MINGGU YANG KETUJUH; PELAJARAN YANG KE-31

The numbers we have had so far have been the simple numbers which grammarians usually call the *cardinal* numbers. Here we have our first examples of *ordinal* numbers, i.e. the numbers which tell us, not how many things there are, but what order they are in. The English ordinal numbers are the series beginning *first, second, third,* etc.

The Malay ordinals can be formed quite simply from the cardinals. We just prefix *yang ke-* to the cardinal to get the ordinal:

tujuh	seven	yang ketujuh	seventh
sebelas	eleven	yang kesebelas	eleventh
dua puluh	twenty	yang kedua puluh	twentieth

The only irregularity is the word for *first,* which is not usually *yang kesatu* but rather *yang pertama. Pertama* is from the Sanskrit word *prathama* which means *first.*

Note too that the ordinal numbers, being true adjectives, always follow the noun to which they are attached:

| buku yang pertama | the first book |
| kapal yang kedua ratus | the two-hundredth ship |

Observe the way in which these numbers are abbreviated in writing: instead of *pelajaran yang ketiga puluh satu* (thirty-first lesson) we can write *pelajaran yang ke-31* (31st lesson).

(94) PUKUL SATU

Pukul really means "strike" or "stroke" and refers to the number of strokes on the gong outside the village police station, which was an old way of indicating time in Malaya. Here again the examples speak for themselves, so study the sentences in Section A carefully.

Seventh Week

Minggu Yang Ketujuh

LESSON 32: TUESDAY

Pelajaran Yang Ke-32: Hari Selasa

A. Sentences

Pukul satu setengah.

Pukul berapa sekarang?

Sekarang pukul enam setengah.

Pukul berapa encik bangun pagi ini?

Pagi ini saya bangun pada pukul tujuh setengah.

Pada pukul berapa encik pergi ke pejabat pagi ini?

Pagi ini saya lambat sikit; sampai ke pejabat pada pukul sembilan setengah.

Encik boléh datang ke rumah saya malam ini? Ada jamuan makan malam.

Half past one.

What time is it now?

It is now half past six.

What time did you get up this morning?

This morning I got up at half past seven.

What time did you go to the office this morning?

This morning I was a bit late; I got to the office at half past nine.

Can you come to my house this evening? (We're) having a dinner party.

Boléhlah. Terima kasih. Pukul berapa encik mahu saya datang ke sana?

Rather! Thanks very much. What time do you want me to get there?

Pada pukul lapan setengah.

At half past eight.

Pada pukul berapa siaran "Speak Malay" dimulaï?

At what time does the "Speak Malay" programme begin?

Siaran "Speak Malay" dimulaï tiap-tiap hari pada pukul enam setengah.

The "Speak Malay" programme begins every day at 6.30.

Malam Sabtu pada pukul sembilan setengah saya nak pergi téngok wayang gambar di pekan.

On Friday evening at 9.30 I'm going to the cinema in town.

Hari Sabtu pada pukul sepuluh pagi saya nak pergi ke Pulau Pinang nak beli barang.

On Saturday morning at ten o'clock I'm going to Penang to do some shopping.

Tiap-tiap malam pada pukul lapan setengah orang Cina itu pergi ke sekolah nak belajar bahasa Melayu.

Every evening at 8.30 that Chinese goes to school to learn Malay.

Berapa lama dia belajar di sana?

How long does he study there?

Sejam setengah; dia balik pada pukul sepuluh.

An hour and a half; he goes home at ten o'clock.

Pada pukul sepuluh setengah dia tidur.	*At half past ten he goes to bed.*
Tiap-tiap hari Ahad dia dengar siaran "Speak Malay" daripada pukul sembilan sampai pukul sembilan setengah pagi.	*Every Sunday morning he listens to the "Speak Malay" programme from nine o'clock until half past nine.*
Bila dia mulaï belajar bahasa Melayu?	*When did he start learning Malay?*
Sembilan bulan dahulu; sekarang dia sangat pandai.	*Nine months ago; now he's very good at it.*

B. Word List

tengah	*middle*	setengah	*(a) half*
lambat	*slow, late*	malam	*night, evening*
siaran	*broadcast* (n); *programme*	mulaï	*begin*
		sekolah	*school*
tiap-tiap	*every*	lama	*long (of time); old (of things)*
berapa lama	*how long*		
		bila	*when*
dengar	*hear; listen to*	jamuan	*party*
pandai	*clever; good at*	jamuan makan malam	*dinner (or lunch) party*

C. Grammar

(95) PUKUL SATU SETENGAH

Notice the way the half-hours are indicated.

(96) MULAÏ

The two dots on the "i" show that it is to be

pronounced as a separate syllable with a glottal stop between the "a" and the "i." These dots, however, are usually omitted in the new spelling.

(97) MALAM SABTU

Friday evening: this is not a misprint! The Muslim day begins at sunset and not at midnight. This means that the period of darkness goes entirely with the *following* period of daylight and is not divided between the preceding and following daylight periods. Be very careful with this or you may find yourself turning up on the wrong evening for a dinner party!

Malays, in their efforts to be polite and helpful to other races, often needlessly complicate matters by using these expressions in the English manner, i.e. they use *malam Sabtu* to mean *Saturday* evening. Therefore when you receive an invitation, especially verbally, from a Malay to an evening function, it would be wise just to make certain which evening he does mean. When he realises that you do know the correct form, he will be delighted.

(98) TIAP-TIAP HARI

Tiap-tiap means *"every "* or *"each"*. Note the following useful expressions:

tiap-tiap hari	*every day*
tiap-tiap malam	*every night* or *every evening*
tiap-tiap pagi	*every morning*
tiap-tiap petang	*every evening* or *every afternoon*
tiap-tiap minggu	*every week*
tiap-tiap bulan	*every month*
tiap-tiap tahun	*every year*

Seventh Week   LESSON 33: WEDNESDAY

Minggu Yang Ketujuh   Pelajaran Yang Ke-33: Hari Rabu

A. Sentences

Pada pukul lapan
  suku.

At a quarter past eight.

Pukul lapan tiga suku.

*A quarter to nine
  (or 8.45).*

Pada pukul lapan
  tiga suku pagi
  kerétapi bertolak
  dari sini nak
  pergi ke Singapura.

*At a quarter to nine in
  the morning the train
  leaves here for
  Singapore.*

Pukul berapa kerétapi
  itu sampai
  ke Singapura?

*What time does that train
  arrive in Singapore?*

Sampai ke sana pada
  pukul sebelas suku
  malam.

It gets there at 11.15 p.m.

Pukul berapa encik
  bangun pagi ini?

*What time did you get up
  this morning?*

Malam semalam saya
  tidur léwat; pagi
  ini saya lambat
  bangun; pagi ini
  saya bangun pada
  pukul tujuh tiga suku.

*Last night I went to bed
  late and so this morning
  I was slow getting
  up; this morning
  I got up at a
  quarter to eight.*

Encik terlambat! Pukul
  berapa encik sampai
  ke pejabat?

*You were late! And what
  time did you get to the
  office?*

Saya sampai pada pukul
  sembilan suku.

I got there at 9.15.

Tuan tak marah?

Wasn't the boss angry?

Tidak marah. Dia sendiri sampai pada pukul sembilan tiga suka.	*No, he wasn't. He got there at 9.45 himself.*
Pukul lapan lima minit.	*Five (minutes) past eight.*
Kerétapi dari Singapura sampai ke sini pada pukul tujuh dua belas minit.	*The train from Singapore arrives here at twelve minutes past seven.*
Keréta itu bertolak dari sini pada pukul tujuh dua puluh tiga minit.	*It leaves here at 7.23.*
Keréta itu berhenti sebelas minit di sini.	*It stops here for eleven minutes.*
Kapalterbang bertolak dari sini pada pukul dua empat puluh minit.	*The aeroplane leaves here at 2.40 (or: at twenty to three).*
Kapalterbang itu sampai ke Hong Kong pada pukul dua belas lima puluh minit malam.	*That aeroplane arrives in Hong Kong at ten to one in the morning.*
Matahari turun (or: masuk) pada pukul enam lima puluh dua minit petang.	*The sun set at 6.52 p.m.*
Matahari terbit pada pukul enam empat puluh minit pagi.	*The sun rose at 6.40 a.m.*

Pada pukul enam
  lima puluh lima minit
  saya bangun sendiri.

*At five to seven I got up
  myself.*

B. Word List

suku	*quarter*	bertolak	*to start; leave;*
léwat	*late; too late*		*set sail; move*
tuan	*lord; master;*		*off*
	boss; sir; Mr	marah	*angry*
dia sendiri	*he himself*	sendiri	*self*
terbang	*fly* (vb.)	saya sendiri	*I myself*
matahari	*sun*	kapalterbang	*aeroplane*
terbit	*rise (sun)*	turun	*go down; come*
	be issued		*down; descend;*
	(book)		*set (sun)*
berhenti	*stop* (vb.)	masuk	*go in; come in;*
			enter; set (sun)

C. Grammar

(99) PADA PUKUL LAPAN SUKU, PUKUL LAPAN TIGA SUKU

Notice the method of indicating "a quarter past" and "a quarter to" the hour. Literally: *at eight strokes (and a) quarter* and *at eight strokes (and) three quarters.*

(100) LÉWAT, LAMBAT

Both these words means "late." The main difference is that *lewat* implies being *too* late to do something or other (here: too late to get to work on time in the morning) whereas *lambat* implies lateness through slowness (here the man was a bit slow and lazy about getting up). You would use *léwat*, for instance, if you were trying to catch a train but arrived so late that you missed it. You would use *lambat* if you had arranged to meet a friend on the station ten minutes before the train left, and you were eight minutes late for the appointment but still in time for both of you to catch the train.

(101) TUAN

The original meaning of *tuan* is "lord" or "master." It is used to refer to any Malay with a title higher than that of Encik. A *haji* (a person who has made the pilgrimage to Mecca) is addressed as *Tuan* or *Tuan Haji;* so is a *Saiyid* (Syed), that is a man claiming descent from the Prophet Muhammad. Certainly any higher person would be called *Tuan.* By courtesy and custom Europeans are usually called *Tuan* by Malays. Indeed, used by itself as *seorang tuan* it has come to mean a European official or business man, hence "boss."

In Indonesia *tuan* has now ousted *encik* and is used as a general word for Mr or Sir, and like *encik* is used as a polite form for *you.* Now that the Federation is independent, there is a definite tendency to imitate the Indonesian usage, and this should be encouraged as it leads to simplicity and equality. The feminine equivalent of *tuan* is *puan.*

(102) PUKUL DUA EMPAT PULUH MINIT

Malay, like English, uses this "time-table" style of expressing minutes before the hour, but, also like English, it has another way which will be discussed in the next lesson.

Seventh Week	LESSON 34: THURSDAY
Minggu Yang Ketujuh	Pelajaran Yang Ke-34: Hari Khamis

A. Sentence

Pukul lima empat   *Five-forty.*
  puluh minit.

Kurang dua puluh minit pukul enam.	*Twenty minutes to six.*
Kurang lima minit pukul empat Ahmad sampai ke rumah saya.	*At five minutes to four Ahmad arrived at my house.*
Kurang dua puluh minit pukul tujuh dia keluar dari rumah saya nak pergi ke pekan.	*At twenty to seven he left my house to go to town.*
Dia kata kepada saya dia nak pergi téngok wayang gambar.	*He told me that he was going to the pictures.*
Saya bertanya pukul berapa wayang dimulaï.	*I asked him what time the picture began.*
Dia menjawab wayang dimulaï pada pukul tujuh suku.	*He replied that the picture was going to begin at 7.15.*
Saya bertanya: Boléh saya pergi sama?	*I asked: Can I go with you?*
Dia menjawab: Boléhlah!	*He replied: Of course you can.*
Saya kata: Nanti sekejap, Encik Ahmad.	*I said: Just wait a moment, Ahmad.*
Lepas itu saya bertanya: Pukul berapa sekarang?	*Then I asked: What time is it now?*
Ahmad kata: Sekarang kurang suku pukul tujuh. Baik kita pergi lekas.	*Ahmad said: It's a quarter to seven now. We'd better hurry.*
Saya menjawab: Baiklah! Saya nak pergi ambil duit sahaja.	*I replied: All right. I'm just going to get some money.*

Kurang sepuluh minit pukul tujuh kita keluar dari rumah saya, naik béca, pergi ke pekan.	*At ten to seven we came out of my house, caught a trishaw and went to town.*
Pada pukul tujuh sepuluh minit kami sampai ke panggung wayang gambar.	*At ten past seven we arrived at the cinema.*
Masa Ahmad bayar dua ringgit kepada orang béca, saya masuk ke panggung beli tikit.	*While Ahmad was giving two dollars to the trishaw man, I went into the cinema and bought the tickets.*
Pada pukul tujuh suku kami duduk di tempat kami.	*At a quarter past seven we were sitting in our places.*
Gambar itu gambar Melayu—sangat baik.	*It was a Malay picture, and a very good one.*
Pada pukul sembilan tiga suku kami keluar dari panggung wayang.	*At a quarter to ten we came out of the cinema.*
Lepas itu kami masuk ke sebuah kedai kopi nak minum kopi.	*Then we went into a café for some coffee.*
Pada pukul sepuluh setengah kami naik béca nak balik.	*At half past ten we got a trishaw to go home.*

B. Word List

keluar	*come out; go out*	bertanya	*ask, inquire*
nanti	*wait*	menjawab	*answer, reply*

lekas	*immediately; quickly*	sekejap	*a moment*
masa	*time; while; when*	pergi lekas	*go at once; hurry*
gambar	*picture, film*	ambil	*take; get; fetch*
tikit	*ticket*	tempat	*place*
		bayar	*pay* (vb.)

C. Grammar

(103) KURANG DUA PULUH MINIT PUKUL ENAM

Literally: *less twenty minutes six o'clock*. This is the standard way of indicating minutes *to* the hour. Notice that in this case the minutes precede the hour whereas in the case of half hours, quarter hours and minutes *past* the hour it is the hour which comes first, followed by the minutes.

(104) AMBIL

Usually pronounced, but seldom written, *ambik*.

(105) MASA

Masa (time) means "when" when "when" means "while". Otherwise use *bila* or *waktu*. Examples:

> *Masa saya téngok dia...*
> While I was looking at him....
> *Bila saya téngok dia...*
> When I saw him...
> *Masa saya di London...*
> When I was in London...
> *Waktu dia datang...*
> When he came...

Seventh Week

Minggu Yang Ketujuh

A. Sentences

Semalam pada pukul
sebelas pagi saya
bekerja di pejabat.

*Yesterday morning at eleven
o'clock I was working
in the office.*

Tiba-tiba seorang ka-
wan saya masuk.

*Suddenly one of my
friends came in.*

Dia kata: Anak
saya nak berkah-
win hari ini; nak
ada kenduri di
rumah saya malam
ini.

*He said: My son is
getting married today;
there's going to be a
party at my house
tonight.*

Dia kata lagi: Encik
boléh datang ke
rumah saya malam
ini? Ada jamuan
makan malam.

*He went on to say: Can
you come to my house
tonight for dinner?*

Saya sangat suka hati.

I was very pleased.

Saya kata: Boléhlah
encik! Terima kasih.

*I said: Of course I can!
Thank you very much.*

Encik Ahmad kata:
Kenduri dimulaï
pada pukul tujuh suku.

*Ahmad said: The party's
going to begin at 7.15.*

Lepas itu dia
keluar; saya
bekerja lagi.

*Then he went out and I
went on working.*

Pada pukul tujuh
lima minit saya
naik keréta saya,
pergi ke rumah Encik
Ahmad.

*At five past seven I got
into my car and went
to Ahmad's house.*

Sampai ke sana, saya téngok ada ramai orang di rumah itu.	*When I got there I saw that there were lots of people in the house.*
Encik Ahmad berdiri di luar rumah nantikan saya.	*Ahmad was standing outside the house waiting for me.*
Dia jemput saya masuk.	*He asked me to come in.*
Pada pukul lapan kita makan nasi. Sangat sedap.	*At eight o'clock we had dinner. It was very good.*
Pada pukul sebelas setengah ada istiadat bersanding.	*At half past eleven was the bersanding (sitting in state) ceremony.*
Pengantin perempuan sangat cantik.	*The bride was very pretty.*
Saya ingat pengantin laki-laki sangat besar hati.	*I think the bridegroom was very proud.*
Pada pukul dua belas saya naik keréta balik ke rumah saya.	*At twelve o'clock I got into my car and went home.*

B. Word List

tiba	*arrive*	tiba-tiba	*suddenly*
berkahwin	*get married; be married*	kenduri	*feast; party*
		hati	*liver*
besar hati	*proud*	suka hati	*pleased*
berdiri	*stand* (vb.); *stand up*	di luar	*outside*
		nantikan	*wait for*
jemput	*ask, invite*	sedap	*tasty; good (of food)*
istiadat	*ceremony*		
bersanding	*sit in state side by side.*	pengantin perempuan	*bride*
		cantik	*pretty, beautiful*

pengantin	*bride; bride-*	pengantin	*bridegroom*
	groom	laki-laki	

C. Grammar

(106) SUKA HATI, BESAR HATI

The Malays, like the Elizabethans, believe that the liver is the seat of emotions. Hence, where we have many similar expressions in English involving the word *heart* the Malays use *hati* instead. Don't be misled into thinking that *hati* means *heart*. The real word for heart is *jantung*. It is *jantung* that you discuss with the doctor and the butcher, but *hati* with your lover!

Further common expressions using *hati:*

sakit hati	*angry*
susah hati	*worried, anxious*
kecil hati	*hurt (feelings)*

(107) SAYA BEKERJA LAGI

I *went on* work*ing*. Note this construction which is very common in colloquial Malay.

So also *dia kata lagi*—he *went on to* say.

(108) NANTI, NANTIKAN

Nanti means *to wait* and *nantikan* means *to wait for*. In other words they are intransitive and transitive respectively.

(109) ISTIADAT BERSANDING

The bersanding ceremony is the focal point of a Malay wedding. The bridal couple are regarded as king and queen for the day, and at some auspicious hour, often very late at night, they sit side by side (bersanding) on a double throne (pelamin) and are honoured by all their friends and relations.

Seventh Week   REVISION LESSON G: WEEK-END

Minggu Yang Ketujuh   Pelajaran Ulangkaji G: Hari Sabtu dan Hari Ahad

A. Sentences

Revise all the sentences in Lessons 31–35.

B. Word List

        ulangkaji   *revision*

Revise all the word lists in Lessons 31–35.

C. Grammar

Revise all the grammar sections (93–109) in Lessons 31–35.

D. Exercises

(1) Make up twenty sentences using what you have learnt.

(2) Read aloud the following narrative, which is a continuation of the story told in Lesson 35, Section A:

Pada pukul dua belas sepuluh minit malam, saya sampai ke rumah saya. Saya mandi; lepas itu saya tidur. Pagi ini saya bangun léwat sikit—pada pukul tujuh tiga suku. Lekas saya mandi, makan roti, minum kopi. Lepas itu saya naik keréta nak pergi ke pejabat. Pada pukul lapan tiga suku saya sampai ke sana; tuan saya sangat marah. Dia berkata (same as *kata*), "Encik datang léwat—suku jam!" Saya kata, "Tuan, malam semalam saya pergi ke rumah seorang kawan saya. Anak dia nak berkahwin. Saya tinggal di rumah dia sampai pukul dua belas malam nak tengok istiadat bersanding. Saya balik lewat ke rumah saya. Saya tidur pada pukul satu malam, lambat sikit bangun pagi ini." Tuan saya orang baik. Dia kata, "Baiklah! Tetapi ada banyak kerja hari ini. Encik boléh tinggal di pejabat sampai pukul tujuh malam?" Saya menjawab, "Boléhlah, tuan."

(3) Translate (2) above into English.

(4) Translate into Malay:

  (a) My daughter is getting married today; there will be a big party in the bridegroom's house.

  (b) Many people will go there to see the bersanding ceremony at ten-thirty.

  (c) My daughter is very pretty; the bridegroom is very pleased.

  (d) I think we shall be going to bed late tonight.

  (e) This lesson is a revision lesson.

  (f) That Indian aeroplane arrived in Singapore at 11.57 p.m. *(malam)*.

  (g) This morning I came late (say: late to come) to the office; my boss was very angry.

  (h) Every day he tries to speak Malay with the Malays in the office; the more he tries, the better he is at speaking.

  (i) My boss is going to England on leave next month.

  (j) I don't know where my book is. Can I look at yours? Of course you can.

A. Sentences

Bapa saya sudah pergi ke Kuala Lumpur.	*My father has gone to Kuala Lumpur.*
Bapa saya belum pergi ke Kuala Lumpur.	*My father has not (yet) gone to Kuala Lumpur.*
Encik sudah beli buah manggis?	*Have you bought any mangosteens?*
Sudah. Saya sudah beli sepuluh biji.	*Yes, I have. I have bought ten.*
Bapa encik sudah beli keréta baharu?	*Has your father bought a new car?*
Belum. Dia belum beli.	*No, he hasn't bought one yet.*
Encik sudah baca suratkhabaı hari ini?	*Have you read the paper today?*
Belum. Saya belum beli suratkhabar hari ini.	*No, I haven't. I haven't bought a paper today yet.*
Orang itu belum mulaï belajar bahasa Melayu.	*That man has not yet begun to learn Malay.*
Orang Cina itu pandai bercakap Melayu.	*That Chinese is good at speaking Malay.*
Setahun dahulu orang Cina itu tak tahu bercakap Melayu, tetapi sekarang dia sudah pandai.	*A year ago that Chinese couldn't speak Malay, but now he's good at it.*

Makanan pagi saya selalu siap pada pukul lapan.	*My breakfast is always ready at eight o'clock.*
Makanan sudah siap, tuan.	*The meal is ready, sir.*
Encik Ahmad selalu sihat.	*Ahmad is always fit.*
Minggu lepas bapa saya sakit; sekarang sudah sihat.	*Last week my father was ill; now he is well.*
Kerja orang itu sangat baik.	*That man's work is very good.*
Mula-mula kerja orang itu tidak baik; sekarang sudah baik.	*At first that man's work was not good; but it's all right now.*
Rumah orang itu selalu sangat kotor.	*That man's house is always very dirty.*
Semalam ada kenduri di rumah saya; pagi ini rumah saya sudah kotor.	*Yesterday there was a party in my house; this morning the house is dirty.*

B. Word List

sudah	*finished, completed*	belum	*not (yet)*
sihat	*fit, well, healthy*	siap	*ready*
kotor	*dirty*	mula-mula	*at first; originally*

C. Grammar

(110) SUDAH PERGI, BELUM PERGI

Sudah before a verb gives the verb more or less the meaning of the English perfect tense (either present, past, or future perfect); i.e. *sudah pergi* according to the context, may mean "has gone," or "will have gone." *Belum* is substituted for *sudah* to give the negative form. Cf. (111).

(111) SUDAH PANDAI

Sudah, with its negative form *belum*, has a slightly different meaning in English though not in Malay, when placed before an adjective. An adjective without *sudah* or *belum* describes a state of affairs which may be considered as permanent, or rather as having existed for some time and likely to continue for a while at least. An adjective preceded by *sudah* describes a state of affairs *which has only just come about; sudah* plus adjective, in other words, describes a new condition which has only just started. E.g.:

Orang Cina itu pandai   *That Chinese is good at*
   bercakap Melayu.   *speaking Malay.*

[Here the plain *pandai* implies that the Chinese in question has always been good at Malay, still is good at it, and presumably always will be: he was probably born in Malacca, for instance.]

Setahun dahulu orang   *A year ago that Chinese*
   Cina itu tak tahu ber-   *couldn't speak Malay,*
   cakap Melayu, tetapi   *but now he's good at it.*
   sekarang sudah pandai.

[Here *sudah pandai* means that our Chinese friend's cleverness is a fairly recent thing. A year ago he was no good at Malay, but since then he must have been working hard at it and has now reached the stage of being good at the language.]

The same difference exists between the other pairs of examples given in the sentences in Section A. Look closely at them and try to see why there is a *sudah* in one case and not in the other.

(112) YANG KEDELAPAN

This form is more common in writing than *yang kelapan*. The student should prefer the written form of the ordinal numbers, since these numbers are not very much used in talking anyway. In spoken Malay *minggu nombor lapan* would be more usual.

Eighth Week

Minggu Yang Kedelapan

LESSON 37: TUESDAY

Pelajaran Yang Ke-37: Hari Selasa

A. Sentences

Hari ini saya nantıkan seorang kawan saya datang.

Today I am waiting for a friend of mine to come.

Semalam dia kata dia nak sampai ke rumah saya pada pukul enam.

Yesterday he said that he would arrive at my house at six o'clock.

Kami sudah bersetuju nak pergi téngok wayang gambar.

We have agreed to go to the pictures.

Tetapi sekarang sudah pukul enam suku; dia belum datang.

But now it is a quarter past six, and he's not yet come.

Ah! Dia sudah datang.

Ah! Here he comes.

Maafkan saya, encik. Saya sudah léwat.

Forgive me. I am late.

Tak apalah. Ada se-tengah jam lagi.

That's all right. We've still got half an hour.

Tetapi saya sudah tuang téh; sekarang kita tak sempat minum.

But I've made some tea, and now we haven't got time to drink it.

Tak sempat? Boléhlah
kita minum.

*No time? Of course we
can drink it.*

Mana boleh? Naik
béca sampai ke
panggung wayang
dua puluh minit!

*How can we? It's twenty
minutes in a trishaw
to the cinema!*

Naik béca? Siapa nak
naik béca?

*In a trishaw? Who's going
in a trishaw?*

Kita nak naik keréta.
Hari ini saya
sudah beli.

*We're going by car. I
bought one today.*

Itu keréta encik? Saya
ingat keréta séwa.

*Is that your car? I
thought it was a taxi.*

Bukan! Saya sudah
menang loteri; sudah
beli sebuah kereta
baharu.

*No, it isn't! I've won a
lottery so I've bought
a new car.*

Baguslah! Encik sudah
menang loteri, boléh
belanja saya.

*Splendid! If you've won
a lottery, you can pay
for me (treat me).*

Boléhlah! Lepas itu
kita nak ke
sebuah kedai makan
nak makan nasi.

*Of course I can! And after
that we'll go to a
restaurant for a meal.*

Terima kasih, encik!

Thank you very much!

Buku ini saya sudah
baca; buku itu
saya tak baca
lagi.

*This book I have read;
that book I have not yet
read.*

Bapa saya tak pergi
ke Singapura lagi.

*My father has not gone
to Singapore yet.*

Gambar "Hang Tuah"
saya tak téngok
lagi.

*I have not yet seen the
picture of "Hang Tuah."*

Kawan encik sudah sampai?	*Is your friend here yet?*
Tidak lagi. Dia nak sampai ésok.	*Not yet. He will arrive tomorrow.*

B. Word List

bersetuju	*agree*	maafkan	*excuse* (vb.);
tuang	*pour out;*		*forgive*
	make (tea)	sewa	*hire*
tuang téh	*make tea*	loteri	*lottery*
tak sempat	*no time to (do)*	belanja	*treat* (vb.)
keréta séwa	*taxi; hire-car*		
menang	*win*		

C. Grammar

(113) TUANG TÉH

This is the correct expression for "make tea". Although *tuang* means "pour out," *tuang téh* does not mean "pour out tea," that would be *bancuh téh*, literally "mix tea," i.e. "mixing the tea, milk and sugar together in the cup." *Bancuh* is also used for making drinks like coffee which are often in powder form and have to be mixed with milk or water before being drunk. Instead of *tuang téh* and *bancuh kopi*, however, one can say *buat téh*, and *buat kopi*.

(114) MANA BOLÉH?

A very common colloquial expression meaning literally something like "how can?", an expression which has become quite common also in Malayan English. It may have many translations in English, such as, "What a ridiculous idea!" "What on earth are you talking about?", "Absolute nonsense" and so on, according to the context and the tone of voice in which it is uttered.

(115) TIDAK LAGI

These two words are often used together in colloquial language instead of the more formal *belum* which is felt by some Malays as being rather bookish.

Eighth Week

Minggu Yang Kedelapan

LESSON 38: WEDNESDAY

Pelajaran Yang Ke-38: Hari Rabu.

A. Sentences

Encik nak pergi ke pasar.	*You are going to the market.*
Adakah encik nak pergi ke pasar?	*Are you going to the market?*
Ya.	*Yes.*
Tidak/Tak.	*No.*
Adakah encik tahu bercakap bahasa Cina?	*Can you speak Chinese?*
Ya. Saya belajar lama di Hong Kong.	*Yes, I can. I studied it for a long time in Hong Kong.*
Adakah encik suka makan daging babi?	*Do you like eating pork?*
Tak. Saya orang Melayu; saya tak boléh makan daging babi.	*No, I don't. I'm a Malay; I can't eat pork.*
Adakah encik nak pergi ke Pulau Pinang?	*Are you going to Penang?*
Ya. Saya nak beli barang di sana.	*Yes, I am. I'm going to do some shopping there.*
Adakah encik sudah beli sebuah kereta baharu?	*Have you bought a new car?*

Tak. Saya tak ada banyak duit tahun ini.	*No, I haven't. I haven't got much money this year.*
Adakah encik duduk di Kuala Lumpur?	*Do you live in Kuala Lumpur?*
Ya. Sudah lima tahun saya duduk di Kuala Lumpur.	*Yes, I do. I've been living in Kuala Lumpur for five years.*
Adakah encik bekerja di pejabat Tuan Brown?	*Do you work in Mr Brown's office?*
Tak. Saya bekerja di pejabat Encik Sulaiman.	*No, I don't. I work in Mr Sulaiman's office.*
Adakah orang itu orang Cina?	*Is that man a Chinese?*
Ya. Dia orang Hokkien.	*Yes, he is. He's a Hokkien.*
Adakah nama orang Cina itu Ah Kau?	*Is his name Ah Kau?*
Tidak. Nama dia Ah Kim.	*No, it isn't. His name is Ah Kim.*
Adakah dia tahu bercakap Melayu?	*Can he speak Malay?*
Ya. Sudah lama dia duduk di Malaysia.	*Yes, he can. He has been living in Malaysia for a long time.*
Adakah dia suka makan gulai yang sangat pedas?	*Does he like eating very hot curry?*
Tidak	*No, he doesn't.*

B. Word List

ya	*yes*
tidak, tak	*no*

C. Grammar

(116) ADAKAH

There are several ways of forming questions in Malay. The easiest of these we have already learnt to use, viz. keep the statement form and raise the voice at the end of the sentence in talking, and write a question mark in writing.

Another easy way is by keeping the statement form but prefixing it with the words *adakah* which literally means something like "is it (true) that...?" (Cf. French questions beginning with *est-ce que.*)

(117) SUDAH LIMA TAHUN SAYA DUDUK DI KUALA LUMPUR: SUDAH LAMA DIA DUDUK DI MALAYSIA

Notice the construction exemplified in these two sentences. *Sudah* may be used even with a noun *(lima tahun)* if the sense permits. Literally these two sentences mean (a) finished five years I live in K.L. and (b) completed long time he live in Malaysia.

Eighth Week

Minggu Yang Kedelapan

LESSON 39: THURSDAY

Pelajaran Yang Ke-39: Hari Khamis

A. Sentences

Dia nak pergi ke Kuala Lumpurkah?	*Is he going to Kuala Lumpur?*
Dia nak baca buku itukah?	*Is he going to read that book?*
Diakah nak baca buku itu?	*Is he going to read that book?*
Dia nak bacakah buku itu?	*Is he going to read that book?*

Dia nak baca buku itukah?	*Is he going to read that book?*
Buku itukah dia nak baca?	*Is that the book he's going to read?*
Encikkah nak beli se-buah keréta baharu?	*Is it you who are going to buy a new car?*
Ikan ini murahkah?	*Is this fish cheap?*
Ikan inikah murah?	*Is this fish cheap?*
Dia datangkah?	*Is he coming?*
Ya. Dia datang.	*Yes, he is.*
Tidak. Dia tak datang	*No, he isn't.*
Bapa diakah nak beli keréta di Singapura?	*Is it his father who's going to buy a car in Singapore?*
Ya. Bapa dia.	*Yes, it is.*
Dia datangkah pada pukul sembilan setengah?	*Is he coming at half past nine?*
Tidak. Tak datang. Dia nak datang pada pukul sepuluh.	*No, he isn't. He is going to come at ten o'clock.*
Pukul sepuluhkah dia nak datang?	*Is it ten o'clock that he's coming?*
Ya. Pukul sepuluh.	*Yes, it is.*
Budak inikah encik téngok di pekan?	*Is this the boy you saw in town?*
Ya. Budak ini.	*Yes, it is.*

B. Word List

kah   question particle

C. Grammar

(118) KAH

Here we have another common method of forming questions in Malay. We simply add *kah* to the end of the sentence, or more accurately we add *kah* to the most important word in the sentence, i.e. the word about which the question is really being asked. Cf. the first batch of examples in Section A. Pay special attention to the English translations of these examples.

Notice too (cf. the last batch of examples) how answers are given to such questions. If the answer is "yes", the word to which the *kah* is added is repeated in the answer with or without other words. The examples given will make this clear. If the answer is "no", the answer will contain *tidak, bukan* or *belum* (or any of their alternative forms) according to the structure of the original statement.

Eighth Week

LESSON 40: FRIDAY

Minggu Yang Kedelapan

Pelajaran Yang Ke-40: Hari Jumaat

A. Sentences

Semalam seorang kawan saya di Kuala Lumpur mati.

Yesterday a friend of mine in Kuala Lumpur died.

Orang itu belum mati.

That man has not yet died— or that man is not yet dead.

Orang itu tidak mati lagi.

— ditto —

Adakah encik sudah baca buku ini?

Have you read this book?

Belum. Saya belum baca.	*No, I haven't read it yet.*
Tak. Saya tak baca lagi.	*— ditto —*
Adakah encik suka makan gulai pedas?	*Do you like eating hot curry?*
Ya. Saya sangat suka makan gulai pedas.	*Yes, I do; I like it very much.*
Adakah encik suka makan buah durian?	*Do you like eating durians?*
Tak. Ramai orang putih tak suka makan durian.	*No, I don't. Many Europeans don't like them.*
Diakah nak datang malam ini?	*Is he coming tonight?*
Ya. Dia nak sampai pukul lapan tiga suku.	*Yes, he is. He'll arrive at a quarter to nine.*
Malam inikah dia nak datang?	*Is it tonight he's coming?*
Ya. Malam ini.	*Yes.*

B. Word List

No new words.

C. Grammar

(119) Revise the grammar of Lessons 36–39 (Grammar sections 110–118).

Eighth Week   REVISION LESSON H: WEEK-END
Minggu Yang Kedelapan   Pelajaran Ulangkaji H: Hari Sabtu dan Hari Ahad

A. Sentences

Revise all the sentences of Lessons 36–40.

B. Word List

Revise all the word lists of Lessons 36–40.

C. Grammar

Revise all the grammar sections (110–118) of Lessons 36–39.

D. Exercises

(1) Make up twenty questions using the three different ways you have learnt and give the answers to them.

(2) Put each of the following statement into question form in three different ways:

(a) Orang itu orang Cina.
(b) Encik tahu bercakap bahasa Tamil.
(c) Bapa dia nak datang ésok.
(d) Emak encik sudah mati.
(e) Dia sudah dapat surat daripada bapa dia.

(3) Read aloud the following conversation:

A. Apa khabar, encik?

B. Khabar baik. Apa khabar bapa encik?

A. Bapa saya sangat sihat, tetapi seorang kawan saya sakit. Dia sudah masuk hospital di Kuala Lumpur. Dia sakit kuat.

A. Orang kata kepada saya bapa encik sakit; apa khabar dia?

B. Khabar sangat baik. Minggu lepas dia sakit kuat; dia masuk hospital di Ipoh, tetapi sekarang dia sudah baik; dia sudah keluar dari hospital nak balik ke rumah. Dia sudah beli sebuah keréta baharu, sekarang dia nak pergi ke Singapura nak bercuti tiga minggu di sana.

A. Baguslah! Di mana dia nak tinggal di Singapura?

B. Dia nak tinggal di rumah seorang kawan saya.

A. Adakah orang itu orang India?

B. Tak. Kawan saya itu orang putih. Dia ada sebuah rumah di pantai; bapa saya boléh berihat (rest) di pantai téngok laut (sea).

A. Dia nak berenangkah?

B. Bapa sayakah? Tidak. Dia tak tahu berenang.

(4) Translate the conversation in (3) into English.

(5) Translate into Malay:

    (a) Can your mother swim? No, she can't.

    (b) Can that Indian speak English? No, he can't. He can only speak Tamil.

    (c) Encik Ahmad's father is dead.

    (d) Has your father bought that big house in Ipoh? No.

    (e) At first he couldn't speak Malay, but last year he went to school every day to learn. Now he is very good at speaking Malay.

    (f) That Chinese has been living in Malaya for a long time but he is no good at (speaking) Malay.

    (g) Malaysia is now independent.

    (h) Gibraltar is not yet independent.

    (i) I have been learning Chinese for three years, but I am not yet good at speaking it.

    (j) Do you like sitting on the beach watching the sea? Yes, I do.

A. Sentences

Orang itu kena denda
seratus ringgit.

*That man incurred a fine
of $100, or, that man was
fined $100.*

Orang itu kena hukum
gantung.

*That man incurred sentence
of hanging, or, that man
was sentenced to be hanged.*

Orang itu sudah kena
tangkap.

*That man has incurred
arrest, or, that man has
been arrested, or, that man
is under arrest.*

Orang itu luka.

That man was wounded.

Orang itu kena hukum
penjara.

*That man was sentenced
to prison.*

Orang itu sudah mati
kena penyakit.

*That man has died of a
disease (lit. has died incurring diseases).*

Jari dia luka kena
pisau.

*His finger is cut with a
knife, or, he's cut his finger
with a knife.*

Orang itu sudah mati
kena langgar keréta.

*That man has been killed
through being knocked down
by a car.*

Saya kena pergi ke
pasar nak beli
barang.

*I must go to the market
to do some shopping, or,
I've got to go to the market
to do some shopping.*

Encik kena beri
dia dua belas ringgit.

*You've got to give him
twelve dollars.*

Kita kena pergi ke pejabat pada pukul lapan setengah pagi.	*We've got to go to the office at half past eight in the morning.*
Suka tak suka dia kena pergi ke pejabat juga.	*Whether he likes it or not, he's got to go to the office.*
Suka tak suka dia kena belajar Inggeris juga.	*Whether he likes it or not, he's got to learn English.*
Suka tak suka kami kena bermalam di Ipoh juga.	*Willy-nilly we had to spend the night in Ipoh.*
Suka tak suka encik kena bekerja juga.	*Whether you like it or not, you've got to work.*
Suka tak suka, bapa saya sudah pergi ke Kuala Lumpur juga.	*Whether he likes it or not, my father has gone to Kuala Lumpur.*

B. *Word List*

kena	*incur, be affected by*	denda	*fine* (n.)
		hukum	*sentence*
kena denda	*be fined*	gantung	*hang*
kena hukum	*be sentenced*	hukum	*sentence of*
kena hukum gantung	*be sentenced to death*	gantung	*death*
kena tangkap	*be arrested*	tangkap	*catch, arrest*
luka	*be wounded*	luka	*wound*
penjara	*prison, gaol*	penyakit	*disease, illness*
jari	*finger*	pisau	*knife*
langgar	*collision*	kena langgar	*be run over*
suka tak suka	*willy-nilly*	keréta	*by a car*
bermalam	*spend the night*	juga	*all the same*

C. Grammar

(120) KENA DENDA

In the first two groups of examples in Section A we meet the word *kena* in its basic meaning, i.e. *incurring* or *being affected by* something. The student will have noticed that the most natural way of translating this meaning into English is by the use of the English *passive voice*. We may almost say that *kena* is used to form the passive in colloquial Malay, especially when the occurrence is something *unpleasant*. Strictly speaking Malay makes no distinction whatever between active and passive in its verb, but it may help the English-speaking student to think of *kena* in this way.

In the third group of examples we see *kena* in its extended meaning of *obligation* or *duty*. Could this perhaps be because duty is so often unpleasant?

In both cases the examples will teach you more than a long explanation; so study them carefully.

(121) SUKA TAK SUKA . . . . (JUGA)

This is a very useful expression which may have various translations in English. *Suka tak suka* is usually followed at the end of the sentence by *juga*, a word to which it is difficult to assign a single meaning in English. In these sentences it means something like *all the same* [whether he likes it or not he's got to go to the office all the same] but it does not really need to be translated into English, although it is necessary in Malay. We shall have more to say about *juga* later; for the moment only use it in this construction and you will not come to grief.

Ninth Week

Minggu Yang Kesembilan

LESSON 42: TUESDAY

Pelajaran Yang Ke-42: Hari Selasa

A. Sentences

Nak ke mana, encik?	*Where are you off to?*
Saya nak ke hospital nak téngok bapa saya.	*I'm off to the hospital to see my father.*
Bapa encik sakitkah?	*Is your father ill?*
Ya. Semalam dia terjatuh tanggá; kaki dia patah.	*Yes. Yesterday he fell downstairs and broke his leg.*
Kasihan dia! Dia kena tinggal lamakah di hospital?	*Poor fellow! Has he got to stay long in hospital?*
Kami tak tahu lagi. Tetapi doktor kata lebih kurang tiga minggu.	*We don't know yet. But the doctor says about three weeks.*
Bapa encik orang tuakah?	*Is your father an old man?*
Bukan tua, bukan muda; dia berumur lima puluh tahun.	*Neither old nor young; he's fifty years old.*
Bagus. Saya ingat tak lama lagi dia baik.	*That's fine. I should think he'll soon be well again.*
Sekarang saya kena pergi ke rumah seorang kawan, tetapi petang ini saya ingat nak pergi téngok bapa encik sendiri, boléhkah?	*Now I've got to go to a friend's house, but this evening I was thinking of going to see your father myself. Will that be all right?*

Boléhlah! Bapa saya
   duduk seorang di
   hospital; dia sangat
   suka hati nak tengok
   encik.

*Of course it will. My
   father's all by himself
   in the hospital; he
   will be delighted to
   see you.*

Pagi tadi saya baca
   dalam suratkhabar,
   seorang pengganas
   kena témbak di
   Negri Sembilan.

*This morning I read in the
   paper that a terrorist
   had been shot in Negri
   Sembilan.*

Sudah matikah dia?

Is he dead?

Sudah. Kalau dia tak
   kena témbak, tentu
   dia kena hukum
   gantung.

*Yes, he is. If he hadn't
   been shot, he would
   certainly have been
   sentenced to be hanged.*

Saya dengar dua orang
   pengganas lagi
   sudah kena tangkap.

*I hear that two other
   bandits were arrested.*

Sudah. Dua orang itu
   sangat muda; nak
   kena hukum
   penjara sahaja.

*Yes, they were; those
   two were very young;
   they'll only be sen-
   tenced to prison.*

Jari encik sakitkah?

*Is there something wrong with
   your finger?*

Sakit. Pagi tadi sudah
   luka kena pisau
   cukur saya.

*Yes. I cut it this morning
   with my razor.*

Baik encik pakai pisau
   cukur elektrik; jari tak
   luka.

*You'd better use an electric
   razor, then you won't
   cut your fingers!*

Pisau cukur elektrik
   sangat mahal —
   saya tak tahan
   belanjanya.

*Electric razors are very
   dear; I can't afford
   one.*

Mahallah; tetapi
  pisau cukur elektrik
  tidak berbahaya.

*Yes, they are; but they're
  not dangerous.*

B. Word List

terjatuh	*fall down*	tangga	*stairs, stair-*
terjatuh	*fall*		*case, ladder*
tangga	*downstairs*	patah	*broken, fractured*
kaki	*leg, foot*	doktor	*doctor*
kasihan	*pity*	muda	*young*
kasihan	*poor*	sekejap	*in a*
dia!	*fellow!*		*moment*
tua	*old (of*	tak lama	
	people)	lagi	*soon*
berumur	*to be aged; to*	petang	*afternoon,*
	be old		*evening*
pengganas	*terrorist,*	témbak	*shoot*
	bandit	Negeri	
negeri	*state (n.),*	Sembilan	*Negri Sembilan*
	country	tadi	*just now*
kalau	*if*	cukur	*shave*
tentu	*certain,*	pisau-	
	certainly	cukur	*razor*
pagi tadi	*this morning*	pakai	*use; wear,*
	(refers to the		*put on*
	past only)	belanja	*expense, cost*
elektrik	*electric*	tahan	*to be able*
tahan	*hold out,*	belanja	*to afford*
	stand, last		
	(vb.), endure		

C. Grammar

(122) TERJATUH TANGGA

Literally: fell the stairs. There is no need for a preposition in such a sentence in Malay. The simple juxtaposition of the two words is sufficient.

(123) TUA-LAMA

Normally *tua* is used with people and *lama* with things. Sometimes however, we find *lama* used with people. It then means "old" in the sense of "previous," "ex-." Examples:

kawan tua	*an old friend (i.e. a friend who is an old man)*
kawan lama	*an old friend (i.e. a friend one has known for a long time, but who may still be young)*
guru lama saya	*my old teacher (i.e. the teacher I had when I was at school)*

(124) PETANG INI

Petang means afternoon and that part of the evening which is still in daylight. Evening after dark is *malam.*

(125) NEGERI SEMBILAN

Literally: Nine States. Negri Sembilan consists of nine small states joined together into one unit. The ruler is elected and is not a Sultan or a Raja; he is called Yang Dipertuan Besar, i.e. *he who has been made the great lord.* Perlis is, ruled by a *Raja,* Malacca and Penang have Governors, and all other states are ruled by sultans. The Paramount Ruler of the whole of Malaysia is called the Yang Dipertuan Agung, i.e. *he who has been made the general lord.* He too is elected, but by the other rulers.

(126) CUKUR

This word is transitive. That is to say, it means "to shave someone else." To shave *oneself* is *bercukur*. Examples:

> *Orang Cina itu sudah cukur dia.*
> That Chinese has shaved him.
> *Tiap-tiap pagi saya bercukur pada pukul tujuh.*
> I shave at seven o'clock every morning.

Ninth Week	LESSON 43: WEDNESDAY
Minggu Yang Kesembilan	Pelajaran Yang Ke-43: Hari Rabu

A. Sentences

Dengan siapa encik nak pergi?	*Who are you going with?*
Siapa nak datang makan malam?	*Who's coming to dinner this evening?*
Apa encik sudah beli hari ini?	*What have you bought today?*
Apa encik nak kata kepada dia?	*What are you going to say to him?*
Buku mana encik sudah baca?	*Which book have you read?*
Di pekan mana dia duduk?	*In which town does he live?*
Ada siapa-siapa dalam rumah itu?	*Is there anybody in that house?*
Ada apa-apa dalam pokét encik?	*Is there anything in your pockets?*
Buku mana-mana encik boléh baca.	*You can read any book.*

Adakah siapa-siapa sudah datang nak téngok encik?	Has anyone come to see you?
Adakah siapa-siapa dalam bilik saya?	Is there anybody in my room?
Adakah apa-apa sudah terjatuh dari meja itu?	Has anything fallen off that table?
Adakah apa-apa dalam poket budak itu?	Is there anything in that boy's pocket?
Dia tak boleh duduk di pekan mana-mana di Negeri Kedah.	He's not allowed to live in any town in Kedah.
Tak ada siapa-siapa di sini sekarang.	There isn't anybody here now.
Hari ini tak ada apa-apa di pasar.	There's nothing in the market today.
Apa ada dalam kotak itu?	What is there in that box?
Tak ada apa-apa dalam kotak itu.	There is nothing in that box.
Buku ini, di kedai mana-mana boleh beli.	You can buy this book in any shop.

B. *Word List*

siapa-siapa	*anyone, anybody*	apa-apa	*anything*
		poket	*pocket*
mana-mana	*any* (adj.)	meja	*table*
bilik	*room; bedroom*	kotak	*(small) box*
Negeri Kedah	*Kedah*		

C. Grammar

(127) SIAPA, APA, MANA

Siapa and *apa* are interrogative pronouns meaning *who (or whom)*, and *what* respectively. *Mana* is an interrogative adjective meaning *which,* and, like all adjectives in Malay, follows its noun.

(128) SIAPA-SIAPA, APA-APA, MANA-MANA

When these interrogative words are reduplicated they lose their interrogative meaning, but retain their grammatical nature, i.e. the first two are still pronouns and the third one remains an adjective.

When doubled in this way they become indefinite pronouns and an indefinite adjective respectively. In this use they are very close in meaning and usage to the English indefinite pronouns and adjectives beginning with *any*. They are alike in usage because they can, as in English, only be used in negative and interrogative sentences. In English, in positive sentences, *any*-words are changed to *some*-words, e.g. we say *someone is coming* not *anyone is coming*. These *some*-words are dealt with differently in Malay.

The examples given in Section A should make the usage of these reduplicated forms clear.

Ninth Week
Minggu Yang Kesembilan

LESSON 44: THURSDAY
Pelajaran Yang Ke-44: Hari Khamis

A. Sentences

Siapa pun tidak
sampai lagi.

Nobody has yet arrived.

Siapa pun tidak tahu
bercakap Melayu di
sini.

*Nobody knows how to
speak Malay here.*

Apa pun tak sedap
di kedai makan itu.

*Nothing is worth eating
in that restaurant.*

Apa pun tak kena
cukai.

*Nothing is dutiable (lit.
nothing incurs duty).*

Di kedai mana pun
tak boléh dapat
buku itu.

*You can't get that book
in any shop (or: in
no shop can you get that
book).*

Di rumah mana pun
tak ada orang
Cina.

*There are no Chinese in
any of the houses.*

Di kedai mana-mana
pun boléh beli
barang itu.

*You can buy those things
in any shop.*

Di mana-mana pun
tak boléh dapat.

*You can't get them
anywhere.*

Siapa-siapa pun boléh
pergi ke Kuala
Lumpur.

*Anybody can go to Kuala
Lumpur.*

Siapa pun tak boléh
pergi ke Singapura
hari ini.

*Nobody can go to Singapore
today.*

Apa-apa pun boléh
pakai nak buat
kerja ini.

*You can use anything you
like to do this job.*

Seorang pun tak ada
dalam rumah itu.

*There isn't a soul inside
that house.*

Hari ini di pasar
sebiji manggis pun
tak ada.

*Today in the market there
isn't a single mango-
steen.*

Lembu in seékor pun belum mati.	*Not one of these cattle has yet died.*
Kalam sebatang pun saya tak ada.	*I haven't got a single pen.*
Rokok sebatang pun dia tak ada.	*He hasn't got a single cigarette.*
Hari ini rokok sebatang pun saya tidak hisap lagi.	*I haven't smoked a single cigarette yet today.*
Kampung itu sudah terbakar; sebuah rumah pun tak ada lagi.	*That village has been burned down; there isn't a single house left.*
Duit dia sudah habis. Satu sen pun tak ada lagi.	*His money's all gone. He hasn't got a cent left.*
Siaran ini sudah habis. Satu minit pun tak ada lagi.	*This programme is over. There isn't a minute left.*

B. Word List

cukai	*duty, tax*	kena	*be dutiable,*
rokok	*cigar, cigarette*	cukai	*be taxable*
		hisap	*to smoke*
sebatang rokok	*a cigar, a cigarette*	terbakar	*to be burned down,, catch fire*
kampung	*village, compound*	pun	*cf.* (129, 130).
habis	*finish, finished*		
sudah habis	*all gone, over*		

C. Grammar

(129) SIAPA PUN TIDAK SAMPAI

The interrogatives *siapa, apa,* and *mana* become equivalent to the English *no-one* (or *nobody*), *nothing* and *no* (adj.) when they are combined with *pun* and any of the various words meaning *not*. Often they may be reduplicated at the same time with no change in meaning. Without the *not* (*tidak,* etc.) they have the same meaning as they do without the *pun,* that is *anyone, anything* and *any*. The examples in Section A will make this clearer than a long explanation here.

(130) SEORANG PUN TAK ADA

Here, *pun* means something like the English *even,* i.e. *even one person there is not*. This idiom is very common; study the examples in Section A carefully, and you will see how it works.

Ninth Week   LESSON 45: FRIDAY

Minggu Yang Kesembilan   Pelajaran Yang Ke-45: Hari Jumaat

A. Sentences

Orang salah itu kena denda dua ratus ringgit.	*The guilty man was fined $200.*
Dua orang pengganas sudah kena hukum gantung.	*Two terrorists have been sentenced to death.*
Dua orang penjahat sudah kena tangkap.	*Two bandits have been arrested.*

Kaki orang itu sudah
luka kena pisau.

*That man has cut his leg
with a knife.*

Pagi tadi hidung saya
luka kena pisau cukur.

*This morning I cut my
nose with a razor.*

Sekarang saya kena
pergi ke pasar nak
beli barang.

*I've got to go to the
market now to do
some shopping.*

Pada pukul lapan dia
kena pergi ke
sekolah belajar
bahasa Melayu.

*At eight o'clock he's got
to go to school to
learn Malay.*

Siapa nak datang pada
pukul sembilan
tiga suku?

*Who's coming at a quarter
to ten?*

Apa dia nak buat
bésok di Singapura?

*What's he going to do to-
morrow in Singapore?*

Di rumah mana dia
duduk sekarang?

*Which house is he living
in now?*

Ada siapa-siapa dalam
rumah encik?

*Is there anybody in your
house?*

Ada apa-apa saya
boléh buat di
Singapura?

*Is there anything I can do
in Singapore?*

Siapa pun tidak mahu
datang ke sekolah ini.

*Nobody wants to come to
this school.*

Apa-apa pun tak ada
di pasar hari ini.

*There's nothing in the
market today.*

Hari ini buku mana-
mana pun boléh
baca.

*Today you can read any
book you like.*

Hari ini sepucuk surat
pun tak ada.

*There wasn't a single
letter today.*

B. Word List

salah	*wrong, guilty*	penjahat	*bandit, terrorist*
hidung	*nose*	pucuk	*cl. for letters*

C. Grammar

(131) Revise the grammar of Lessons 41–44.

Ninth Week   REVISION LESSON I: WEEK-END

Minggu Yang Kesembilan   Pelajaran Ulangkaji I: Hari Sabtu dan Hari Ahad

A. Sentences

Revise all the sentences in Lessons 41–45.

B. Word List

Revise all the word lists in Lessons 41–45.

C. Grammar

Revise all the grammar sections (120–130) in Lessons 41–44.

D. Exercises

(1) Make up twenty sentences using what you have already learnt.

(2) Read aloud the following conversation:

A. Adakah encik sudah baca suratkhabar hari ini?

B. Ada. Saya baca ada dua orang pengganas sudah kena témbak di Negeri Selangor; dua orang lagi sudah kena tangkap.

A. Dua orang lagi itu nak kena hukum apa?

B. Tak tahu lagi. Saya ingat dua orang itu nak kena hukum gantung. Dua orang itu bukan orang muda.

A. Ada apa-apa lagi dalam suratkhabar hari ini?

B. Adalah. Ada sebuah kampung terbakar. Sebuah rumah pun tak ada lagi. Seratus orang luka. Ramai orang sudah masuk hospital.

A. Di manakah kampung itu?

B. Saya sudah terlupa (forget). Saya ingat kampung itu di mana-mana di Negeri Kelantan.

A. Kasihan orang kampung itu!—Apa lagi ada dalam suratkhabar?

B. Saya sudah baca, ada seorang kawan saya di Ipoh sudah berkahwin semalam. Istiadat bersanding dia sangat bagus. Apa-apa lagi tak ada hari ini.

(3) Translate the conversation in (2) into English.

(4) Translate into Malay:

   (a) That old man has been fined $200. Poor fellow!

   (b) Have you anything to declare? (Say: have you anything incurring duty?)

   (c) No, not one of these things is dutiable.

   (d) His father has been run over and killed by a car.

   (e) Five terrorists have been sentenced to death; three more have been sentenced to gaol.

   (f) Yesterday in Selangor not one terrorist was arrested.

   (g) I couldn't buy that book anywhere.

   (h) Not one of these durians is tasty.

   (i) In this village not one person can speak Malay.

   (j) There is nothing in that box.

   (k) In this box there are fifty cigarettes.

   (l) I haven't got a single cigarette left.

  (m) She hasn't received a single letter today.

   (n) There is nobody in my room.

   (o) He has cut his nose with a razor.

A. Sentences

Di atas méja ini
   ada lima buah
   buku.

*On this table there are
   five books.*

Kucing itu sudah naik
   ke atas méja saya.

*The cat has climbed on
   to my table.*

Buku saya sudah terjatuh
   dari atas méja.

*My book has fallen off the
   table.*

Rumah orang itu ada
   di atas sebuah
   gunung tinggi.

*That man's house is on
   top of a high
   mountain.*

Kerétapi ini tidak boléh
   naik ke atas gunung
   itu.

*This train can't climb to
   the top of that
   mountain.*

Orang ini sudah mati
   terjatuh dari atas
   bangunan tinggi itu.

*This man was killed by
   falling from the top
   of that high building.*

Di bawah méja ini
   ada seékor kucing.

*Under this table there
   is a cat.*

Kucing itu berlari
   ke bawah méja nak
   tangkap seékor
   tikus.

*That cat ran under the table
   to catch a mouse.*

Sekarang tikus itu sudah
   berlari dari bawah
   méja; kucing nak
   ikut.

*Now the mouse has run
   from under the table;
   and the cat's going
   to follow him.*

Tikus sudah berlari ke belakang sebuah almari besar.

The mouse has run behind a big cupboard.

Sekarang dia bersembunyi di belakang almari itu.

Now he's hiding behind the cupboard.

Kucing sudah nampak; tikus berlari dari belakang almari.

That cat's seen him; the mouse has run from behind the cupboard.

Sekarang kucing duduk di belakang almari dan tikus duduk di depan.

Now the cat's sitting behind the cupboard and the mouse's sitting in front (of it).

Lambat-lambat kucing datang dari belakang ke depan almari.

Slowly the cat is coming from behind to the front of the cupboard.

Sekarang tikus itu takut; sudah lari dari depan almari.

Now the mouse is frightened; he's run away from the front of the cupboard.

Tikus itu sudah naik ke atas méja; kucing cari di bawah; tapi tak boléh nampak tikus.

The mouse has climbed on to the table; the cat's looking for him underneath, but he can't see him.

Sekarang tikus sudah lompat dari atas méja, masuk ke dalam lobang dia.

Now the mouse has jumped off the table and gone into his hole.

Dari dalam lobang dia, dia boléh nampak kucing.

From inside his hole, he can see the cat.

Di dalam lobang tikus itu selamat.

Inside his hole the mouse is safe.

B. Word List

atas	*top*	di atas	*on the top*
ke atas	*to the top (of),*		*(of), on*
	on to	dari atas	*from the top*
gunung	*mountain*		*(of), off*
bawah	*underneath* (n.)	tinggi	*tall, high*
lari	*run away*	berlari	*run*
ikut	*follow; accord-*	tikus	*rat, mouse*
	ing to	belakang	*back, behind* (n.)
bersembunyi	*hide* (intrans.)	almari	*cupboard*
lambat-		depan	*front*
lambat	*slowly*	takut	*fear* (vb.), *be*
lobang	*hole*		*afraid, frightened*
		lompat	*jump*
		selamat	*safe*

C. Grammar

(132) ATAS, BAWAH, BELAKANG, DEPAN

The easiest way to deal with these words, and several others like them which we shall learn in the course of the next few lessons, is to think of them as nouns rather than as prepositions. They then mean "top", "underside", "back" and "front" respectively. They *can* be used by themselves, especially in colloquial speech, as if they were prepositions indicating position. Examples:

atas méja	*on the table*
bawah almari	*under the cupboard*
belakang rumah	*behind the house.*
depan saya	*in front of me*

but more correctly they should always be used with one of the three prepositions, *ke, di, dari.* The choice of preposition is quite easy to make. When the meaning is that of "rest", "staying still in one place", the correct

> *di atas méja ada tiga buah buku*
> on the table are three books
> *di bawah almari ada seékor tikus*
> under the cupboard is a mouse

When motion towards something is implied, the correct preposition is *ke :*
> *dia pergi ke belakang rumah*
> he went (to) behind the house
> *saya masuk ke dalam rumah*
> I went into the house

Note carefully the difference between
> *dia berjalan ke belakang rumah*
> he walked behind (i.e. to the back) of the house

and
> *dia berjalan-jalan di belakang rumah*
> he was walking (about) behind the house (i.e. he
> could not be seen from the front)

The use of *dari* is more obvious to English speakers because we normally use *from* in the same way. Notice however:
> *saya ambil buku dari atas méja*
> I took the book from (the top of) the table
> *buku terjatuh dari atas méja*
> the book fell *off* the table

Bearing all this in mind the student will see that the real meanings of these words, *atas, bawah,* etc. are really those of nouns, i.e. *di atas* means "on the top (of)", *ke atas* means "to the top (of)", and *dari atas* really means "from the top (of)", and so on in the case of the other variable prepositions, as we may call them for want of a better word. When putting English into Malay, we must first of all consider very carefully the exact meaning of the English. We must ask ourselves whether rest, motion towards or motion away from is meant by the English preposition. It will then be quite easy for us to pick the right form in Malay.

Tenth Week

Minggu Yang Kesepuluh

LESSON 47: TUESDAY

Pelajaran Yang Ke-47: Hari Selasa

A. Sentences

Di sebelah rumah saya ada sebuah kedai kopi.

By the side of (next door to) my house there is a coffee shop.

Dia berjalan ke sebelah rumah itu.

He is walking towards the side of that house.

Orang itu sudah berpindah dari sebelah rumah kami.

That man has moved from beside (from next door to) our house.

Di antara dua buah rumah ini ada sebuah kedai makan.

Between these two houses there is a restaurant.

Keréta dia sudah berada di antara dua buah bas.

His car has gone in between two buses.

Sebuah keréta besar sudah keluar dari antara dua buah rumah itu.

A big car has come out from between those two houses.

Keréta dia sudah berhenti di tengah jalan.

His car has stopped in the middle of the road.

Seorang mata-mata sudah pergi ke tengah jalan nak bercakap dengan dia.

A policeman has gone into the middle of the road to speak to him.

Mata-mata itu sudah suruh dia bawa keréta dari tengah jalan.

The policeman has told him to drive his car away from the middle of the road.

Sekarang dia bawa keréta ke tepi jalan.

Now he's driving the car to the side of the road.

Keréta sudah berhenti di tepi jalan.

The car has stopped at the side of the road.

Mata-mata itu sangat marah; dia bercakap dengan orang itu.

The policeman is very angry; he's talking to the man.

Sekarang mata-mata itu tulis nama orang itu ke dalam bukunya.

Now the policeman is writing the man's name in his book.

Sekejap lagi mata-mata itu bagi dia bawa keréta dari tepi jalan.

After a little while the policeman let him drive his car away from the side of the road.

Saya ingat orang itu nak kena denda.

I think the man will be fined.

Saya duduk di Pulau Pinang dengan bapa saya.

I live in Penang with my father.

Dia nak potong roti ini dengan pisau besar.

He's going to cut this bread with a big knife.

Semalam saya bercakap dengan dia di pejabat.

Yesterday I was talking with him (or to him) in the office.

Dengan siapa encik nak pergi téngok wayang gambar?

Who are you going to the pictures with?

Saya nak pergi dengan   *I'm going with a friend*
  seorang kawan saya.   *of mine.*

B. Word List

sebelah	*beside, next door*	berpindah	*move (house)*
	to, next to	antara	*between, among*
bas	*bus*	tengah	*middle*
berhenti	*stop* (vb.)	suruh	*tell, order,*
mata-mata	*policeman*		*command*
bawa	*bring, carry, lead,*	bawa	
	take (a person)	keréta	*drive a car*
tepi	*side, edge*		

C. Grammar

(133) SEBELAH, TEPI, TENGAH

These are all variable prepositions and are treated just like those we studied in (132) in Lesson 46, q.v.

(134) BAS

Bas is, of course, just a phonetic spelling of the English word, "bus".

(135) DENGAN

Dengan is a genuine preposition and as such invariable. Notice that it is always used after *bercakap* and translates either *to* or *with* in the English.

Tenth Week   LESSON 48: WEDNESDAY

Minggu Yang Kesepuluh   Pelajaran Yang Ke-48: Hari Rabu

A. Sentences

Orang itu pandai, tak
    mahu bekerja juga.

*Although that man is clever,
    he doesn't want to work (or:
    That man is clever, (but) he
    doesn't want to work all the
    same).*

Orang itu orang Cina,
    pandai bercakap
    Melayu juga.

*Although that man is a
    Chinese, he is very
    good at speaking Malay.*

Tak ada orang téngok
    dia, dia bekerja
    juga.

*Although no one was looking
    at him, he was
    working.*

Kopi itu tak ada
    gula, dia minum
    juga.

*Although there isn't any
    sugar in the coffee,
    he's drinking it (all the
    same).*

Budak ini tahu bercakap
    Melayu, tak mahu
    bercakap juga.

*Although this boy can
    speak Malay, he doesn't
    want to.*

Dia tak mahu pergi
    téngok guru besar,
    pergi juga.

*Although he didn't want
    to go and see the
    headmaster, he did go all
    the same.*

Dia duduk di Malaysia
    tiga hari sahaja,
    tahu bercakap bahasa
    Melayu pula!

*Although he's been in
    Malaysia only three days,
    he can speak
    Malay!*

Dia budak kecil, tahu
    bercakap lima bahasa
    pula!

*Although he's only a little
    boy, he can (actually)
    speak five languages!*

Orang itu tidak salah, kena denda pula!	*Although that man wasn't guilty, he got fined!*
Budak ini tak belajar, lulus dalam peperiksaan pula!	*Although this boy didn't study, he passed the examination!*
Budak ini tak suka bermain bolasépak pula!	*Just imagine! This boy doesn't like playing football!*
Orang Cina itu pandai bercakap bahasa Tamil pula!	*That Chinese is good at speaking Tamil. Fancy that!*
Orang perempuan ini tak suka pakai pakaian cantik pula!	*This woman doesn't like wearing pretty clothes. Would you believe it!*
Boléhkah saya bercuti bésok, tuan? Boléh juga.	*Can I have the day off to-morrow, sir? Well, yes, I suppose so.*
Encik mahu pergi téngok wayang gambar? Mahu juga.	*Do you want to go to the pictures? Well, yes, I don't mind.*
Makanan ini sedap juga.	*This food isn't bad (i.e. it's quite good).*
Budak ini pandaikah? Pandai juga.	*Is this boy clever? Yes, he is quite bright, I suppose.*

B. Word List

gula	*sugar*	guru besar	*headmaster*
pula	*cf. (137) and (138)*	lulus dalam	*pass (exams)*
		bermain	*play (vb.)*
peperiksaan	*examination*	bola	*ball*
sépak	*kick*	bolasépak	*football*
pakaian	*clothes, clothing*		

C. Grammar

(136) ORANG ITU PANDAI, TAK MAHU BEKERJA JUGA

Notice this idiomatic way of rendering the English *although*. There are other ways, but this is the commonest in conversation. The English although-clause becomes the main clause in the Malay sentence, and *juga* is tacked on to the end of what would be the main clause in English. We do something very similar in colloquial English when we use the words *all the same* or *after all*. The examples in Section A should be studied carefully; they will be clearer than a long explanation.

(137) ORANG ITU TIDAK SALAH, KENA DENDA PULA!

Pula is used in place of *juga* in the construction dealt with in (136) above, when the clause containing it expresses considerable surprise or indignation. Cf. the examples in Section A.

(138) BUDAK INI TAK SUKA BERMAIN BOLASÉPAK PULA!

Pula at the end of a sentence without any although-clause simply expresses great surprise or indignation. It has no precise equivalent in English; one just chooses something that seems to suit the context, e.g. "fancy that!" "just imagine!" and so on. Look carefully at the examples in Section A.

(139) BOLÉH JUGA

Juga, added in this way to a word, has what might be called a softening effect on the meaning. Especially when the resulting sentences is the answer to a question, it suggests a certain reluctance on the part of the speaker. If you ask your Malay teacher whether you can say so and so in Malay, and he says, "Boléh" or "Boléhlah", you are quite safe in doing what you suggest because it will be right. If, on the other hand, he says "Boléh juga", he means something like, "Well, I suppose you could because you're not a Malay; but no Malay would ever say that because it is wrong and sounds very stupid!" He would be far too polite ever to say that in so many words. So, if you are wise, you will treat "boléh juga" in such circumstances as if it were identical in meaning with "tidak boléh".

Once again, the examples in Section A speak louder than words. Study them carefully and try to get the feel of *juga* from them.

(140) LULUS DALAM PEPERIKSAAN
One usually passes *in* an examination in Malay.

Tenth Week

Minggu Yang Kesepuluh

LESSON 49: THURSDAY

Pelajaran Yang Ke-49: Hari Khamis

A. Sentences

Orang itu sakit teruk, mahu pergi bekerja pula!

Although that man is seriously ill he still insists on going to work!

Orang itu kena témbak, tak mati pula!

That man got shot, but he's not dead.

Orang itu kena lang-gar keréta, balik berjalan kaki pula!

That man was run over by a car, but he walked home all the same!

Guru besar suruh dia tulis karangan, dia tak tulis juga.

Although the headmaster told him to write an essay, he didn't write one.

Budak ini bekerja kuat, tak lulus dalam peperiksaan juga.

Although this boy worked hard, he didn't pass the examination.

Boléhkah saya pinjam seratus ringgit daripada encik?

Can I borrow a hundred dollars from you?

Boléh juga. Tetapi saya bukan orang kaya; orang miskin.

Well, yes, I suppose you can. But I'm not a rich man, I'm poor.

Buku ini saya tak mahu lagi; boléhkah saya beri kepada encik?

I don't want this book any more; can I give it to you?

Boléhlah. Terima kasih. Lama saya ingat nak baca buku itu.

You certainly can! Thank you very much. I've been thinking of reading that book for a long time.

Apa ada di dalam semua kotak besar itu?

What's in all those big boxes?

Di dalam kotak itu ada semua barang saya.

In those boxes is all my luggage.

Masa saya bercuti, saya simpan semua barang di dalam kotak besar.

While I was on leave, I put all my things away in big boxes.

Sekarang saya sudah balik nak bekerja di sini.

Now I have come back to work here.

Baik kita buka kotak ini dahulu.

We'd better open this box first.

Semua buku saya ada di dalam.

It's got all my books in.

Eh! Air sudah masuk
ke dalam kotak; buku
sudah basah!

*Oh dear! Water has got
into the box and the
books are wet!*

Saya simpan di tempat
kering, sudah basah
juga!

*Although I put them in
a dry place, they've got
wet all the same!*

Kotak itu di sana
sudah basahkah?

*Has that box over there
got wet?*

Basah juga. Tetapi kotak
itu tak apa; ada
pinggan mangkuk
sahaja di dalam.

*A bit wet. But that box
doesn't matter; it's only
got crockery in it.*

Ada tiga buah kotak
lagi; sudah
basahkah?

*There are three other
boxes; have they
got wet?*

Belum. Air tak sampai
kotak itu.

*No. The water didn't
reach those boxes.*

Mujurlah! Semua pakaian
saya ada di
dalam tiga buah
kotak itu.

*That's lucky! All my
clothes are in those
three boxes.*

B. Word List

teruk	*acute, severe, arduous*	sakit teruk	*seriously ill*
		berjalan	*to walk, go*
karangan	*essay, composition*	kaki	*on foot*
		kuat	*strong*
bekerja kuat	*work hard*	kaya	*rich*
pinjam		semua	*all*
daripada	*borrow from*	simpan	*put away; keep, store (vb.)*
miskin	*poor*		
kotak	*(big) box, crate*		

buka	*open* (vb.)	éh!	*oh dear!*
dahulu	*first* (adv.)	kering	*dry*
basah	*wet*	mangkuk.	*bowl*
pinggan	*plate, dish*	mujur	*lucky,*
pinggan			*fortunate*
mangkuk	*crockery*	mujurlah!	*that's lucky!*

C. *Grammar*

(141) BERJALAN KAKI

Although *berjalan* is very often used by itself to mean *walk,* its real meaning is *to be under way* and can be used of vehicles in motion. Example:

Keréta berjalan cepat. *The car is going fast.*

When there is any emphasis on the *walking* idea, the word *kaki* (foot) is usually added. In the sentence given in Section A above, there is considerable surprise shown that a man run over by a car should be able to return home on his own two feet. Hence the sentence is made more emphatic by adding both *kaki* and *pula.*

(142) PINJAM/PINJAMKAN

Lend is either *Pinjamkan,* which is a bit bookish, or more colloquially, *bagi pinjam.* Examples:

Boléhkah encik pinjamkan saya seratus ringgit? or
   Boléhkah encik bagi saya pinjam seratus ringgit?
Can you lend me a hundred dollars?

(143) BAGI

In addition to its meaning of *give, bagi* is also used to render the English *let, allow, make,* etc. in the formation of what grammarians like to call causative verbs. A few examples will suffice:

bagi dia datang	*let him come*
bagi dia tulis surat	*make him write a letter*

bapa dia bagi dia pergi ke sekolah	*his father sent him (i.e. made him go) to school*
bagi saya pergi téngok wayang gambar	*allow me to go to the pictures*

Bagi pinjam [cf. (142)], therefore, really means, not *lend*, but *allow to borrow*, which comes to the same thing.

The above examples are very colloquial and in more careful Malay *bagi* in such sentences may be substituted by other verbs, according to the context, such as *suruh*, "order, tell", and *biar*, "let, allow", e.g.

Biar dia datang.	*Let him come.*
Suruh dia tulis surat.	*Make him write a letter*
Bapanya suruh dia pergi ke sekolah.	*His father made him go to school*
Biar saya pergi téngok wayang gambar	*Let me go to the pictures.*

(144) SEMUA

Although this word would be regarded as an adjective in English, it is not so regarded in Malay. It is a noun or pronoun meaning something like "the totality of", and for this reason it goes in front of its noun, and does not follow as an adjective would.

Tenth Week

Minggu Yang Kesepuluh

Pelajaran Yang Ke-50 Hari
Jumaat

A. Sentences

Di dalam kotak ini
ada sepuluh batang
rokok.

*In this box there are ten
cigarettes.*

Siapa bubuh rokok itu
ke dalam kotak?

*Who put those cigarettes
into the box?*

Saya nak ambil sebatang
rokok dari dalam
kotak.

*I'm going to take a
cigarette from the box.*

Di atas méja ini
ada tiga buah
buku besar.

*On this table there are
three big books.*

Sebuah buku lagi sudah
terjatuh dari atas
méja.

*One more book has fallen
off the table.*

Sekarang buku itu ada
di bawah méja.

*The book is now under the
table.*

Saya nak ambil buku
itu dari atas
lantai.

*I'm going to pick up the
book from the floor.*

Di sebelah rumah kita
ada sebuah kedai buku.

*By the side of our house
is a bookshop.*

Di tepi jalan kami
duduk ada parit
besar.

*By the side of the road we
live in is a large
drain.*

Di dalam parit itu
ada banyak air.

*In the drain there is a lot
of water.*

Semalam ada seorang
budak Cina terjatuh
ke dalam parit.

*Yesterday a Chinese boy
fell into the drain.*

Budak itu terjatuh ke dalam parit, tidak luka juga.

Although the boy fell into the drain, he wasn't hurt.

Budak itu budak kecil, dia tahu berenang juga.

Although he was a little boy, he knew how to swim.

Pakaian dia sudah basah, badan dia tak luka juga.

Although his clothes got wet, his body wasn't harmed.

Orang India ini tidak pandai, tahu bercakap bahasa Cina pula!

Although this Indian isn't clever, he can speak Chinese!

Boléhkah saya bercuti lima hari? Boléh juga.

Can I have five days' leave? Yes, I suppose so.

Boléhkah saya jemput encik makan malam di rumah saya?

Can I invite you to dinner in my house?

Boléhlah! Terima kasih. Apa kita nak makan?

Rather! Thank you very much. What are we going to eat?

Kita nak makan makanan Melayu; encik suka makankah?

We're going to have Malay food; do you like it?

Suka juga; tetapi saya lagi suka makan makanan Cina.

Yes, I do quite like it; but I prefer Chinese food.

B. Word List

bubuh	*put*	lantai	*floor*
parit	*ditch, drain*	badan	*body*
lagi suka	*prefer*		

C. Grammar

(145) Revise the grammar of Lessons 46–49.

Tenth Week

REVISION LESSON J: WEEK-END

Minggu Yang Kesepuluh

Pelajaran Ulangkaji J: Hari Sabtu dan Hari Ahad

A. Sentences

Revise all the sentences of Lessons 46–50.

B. Word List

Revise all the word lists of Lessons 46–50.

C. Grammar

Revise all the grammar sections (132–144) of Lessons 46–49.

D. Exercises

(1) Make up thirty sentences using what you have learnt so far, and especially what you have learnt in Lessons 46–50.

(2) Read aloud the following brief conversation:

A. Encik sakitkah? Semalam encik tak datang ke pejabat.

B. Sakit juga. Semalam saya berjalan di tepi jalan; tiba-tiba datang sebuah keréta besar; saya tak nampak, terjatuh ke dalam parit.

A. Kelmarin ada banyak air di dalam parit. Pakaian encik sudah basahkah?

B. Sudah. Badan saya tak luka juga. Tetapi doktor kata baik saya tinggal di rumah, nak tidur semalam. Saya tak mahu datang ke pejabat.

(3) Translate the conversation in (2) into English.

(4) Translate into Malay:

(a) Although that man is an Indian he is very good at speaking Chinese.

(b) This Chinese boy doesn't like eating pork, would you believe it?

(c) Although the mouse ran into his hole under the cupboard, the cat caught him

(d) Do you like English food? I don't mind it; but I prefer Malay food.

(e) Would you like to go to the pictures? Would I!? I haven't been to the pictures for a long time. Thank you very much.

(f) I've put fifty cigarettes in this box. Do you want to smoke?

(g) My father is very old; he doesn't like to see women smoking cigarettes.

(h) Although his mother is an old woman she smokes fifty cigarettes a day!

(i) Although Malay curry is very hot, many Europeans like eating it.

(j) Is that curry hot? Yes, I suppose it is rather.

A. Sentences

Pergi tengok apa orang itu buat!	*Go and see what that man is doing!*
Selalu bercakap Melayu!	*Always speak Malay!*
Téngok! Orang itu sudah terjatuh dari atas bumbung rumah itu.	*Look! That man has fallen off the roof of that house.*
Siapa orang itu? Bawa dia kepada saya.	*Who is that man? Bring him to me.*
Mari ke sini! Saya nak bercakap dengan encik.	*Come here! I want to talk to you.*
Mari ke rumah saya pada pukul lima setengah.	*Come to my house at half past five.*
Jangan bercakap dengan orang itu.	*Don't speak to that man.*
Mari lekas. Jangan léngah di sini.	*Come on quickly. Don't hang about here.*
Jangan datang pada pukul empat; datang pada pukul lima.	*Don't come at four o'clock; come at five.*
Pergilah ke rumah dia, jemput dia ke rumah kita untuk makan malam.	*Just go to his house, and ask him to our house for dinner.*
Marilah ke rumah saya pada pukul sembilan setengah.	*Do come to my house at half past nine.*
Janganlah pergi sekarang; kita belum makan malam.	*Oh, don't go now: we haven't had dinner yet.*

Janganlah bercakap bahasa Cina dengan orang ini; dia tak tahu bercakap bahasa Cina.	*Oh, don't speak Chinese to this man; he can't speak Chinese.*
Janganlah pakai baju lama itu; belilah baju baharu.	*Don't wear that old coat; buy a new one.*
Baik encik pergi ke Singapura bésok.	*You'd better go to Singapore tomorrow.*
Baik encik jangan pergi téngok wayang gambar.	*You'd better not go to the pictures.*
Baik kita selalu bercakap Melayu sahaja.	*We'd better always speak Malay only.*
Baik encik jangan beli keréta baharu; encik tak cukup duit.	*You'd better not buy a new car; you haven't got enough money.*

B. Word List

bumbung	*roof*	jangan	*don't*
léngah	*idle* (vb.); *hang about*	baju	*coat, jacket, blouse*
		cukup	*enough, sufficient, to have enough*

C. Grammar

(146) GIVING ORDERS IN MALAY

There are many ways of giving orders in Malay, and we shall now begin to deal with them in ascending order of politeness. Each new form should be thought of as more polite than the preceding one.

    (a) The simplest and most direct way to give a command is to use the plain and simple verb without any additions:

        pergi!   *go!*

beli baju baharu!	*buy a new coat!*
bawa dia ke sini!	*bring him here!*

The negative of this (English *don't*) is formed by placing *jangan* before the verb:

jangan pergi!	*don't go!*
jangan beli keréta!	*don't buy a car!*
jangan makan!	*don't eat (it)!*

The only exception to this rule is the verb *datang*, which many Malays use in commands only when negative; in the positive form the word *mari* is usually substituted by such speakers:

mari ke sini!	*come here!*
jangan datang malam ini!	*don't come tonight!*

In this connexion cf. (41) in Lesson 14.

(b) The force of a command is softened slightly, and thereby made more polite, if we add to the verb, when the command is positive, and to the *jangan,* when the command is negative, the particle *-lah.*

pergilah!	*oh, do go!*
marilah ke rumah saya!	*do come to my house!*
janganlah léngah!	*oh, don't hang about!*

(c) Politer still is the form we have already learned in (39) in Lesson 14, viz. prefixing the word *baik* to the verb; the negative of this is *baik jangan:*

Baik éncik pergi ke Tanjung.	*You'd better go to Penang.*
Baik jangan tulis surat itu.	*You'd better not write that letter.*

Study the examples in Section A above and try to feel the difference between the various forms. We shall discuss still more polite form in the next lesson.

Eleventh Week
Minggu Yang Kesebelas

A. Sentences

Marilah kita bercakap Melayu hari ini.	*Come on, let's speak Malay today.*
Marilah kita pergi téngok wayang gambar di pekan.	*Come on, let's go to the pictures in town.*
Marilah kita berbual-bual.	*Come on, let's have a chat.*
Marilah kita makan nasi di kedai makan itu.	*Come on, let's eat in that restaurant.*
Marilah kita pergi ke mesjid nak sembah-yang.	*Come on, let's go to the mosque for prayers.*
Encik boléh datang ke rumah saya petang ini?	*Please come to my house this afternoon* (or, of course: *can you come to my house this afternoon?).*
Boléh cuci keréta saya hari ini?	*Clean my car today, will you please?*
Boléh, tuan.	*Yes, sir.*
Boléh bawa saya segelas air sejuk? Boléh, tuan.	*Please bring me a glass of cold water. Yes, sir.*
Tak payah buat kerja itu hari ini.	*There is no need to do that job today.*
Tak payah pergi ke kedai itu; bésok saya nak pergi sendiri.	*Don't bother to go to that shop; I'll go myself tomorrow.*
Tak payah tuang téh sekarang; saya nak keluar.	*Don't bother to make tea now; I'm just going out.*

Tak payah tulis surat
kepada dia; bésok
dia nak datang
sendiri.

Don't bother to write him a letter; he's coming himself tomorrow.

Jangan tidak bercakap
Melayu di rumah itu.

Whatever you do, don't fail to speak Malay in that house.

Jangan tidak datang
ke rumah saya pada
pukul sembilan.

At all costs come to my house at nine o'clock.

Jangan tidak pergi
téngok Tokong Ayer
Itam di Pulau
Pinang.

Don't miss going to see the Ayer Itam Temple in Penang.

Jangan sekali-kali pergi
ke rumah orang itu.

Whatever you do, don't go to that man's house.

Jangan sekali-kali masuk
seorang ke dalam hutan.

Don't ever go into the jungle by yourself.

Jangan sekali-kali buka
kotak itu di sana.

Don't open that box over there, whatever happens.

Masa encik datang dari
Ipoh ke Alor
Setar, jangan tidak
singgah di rumah
saya di Kuala
Kangsar.

When you are coming from Ipoh to Alor Star, don't forget to call in at my house in Kuala Kangsar.

Jangan tidak dengar
siaran "Speak Malay"
tiap-tiap hari
pada pukul enam
setengah.

Don't fail to listen to the "Speak Malay" programme every day at 6.30.

B. Word List

berbual-bual *have a chat*   cuci   *clean* (vb.)

gelas	*glass*	sejuk	*cold*
tak payah	*there's no need,*	sekali	*once*
	don't bother	jangan	
seorang	*alone, by*	sekali-kali	*don't ever*
	oneself	singgah	*call in,*
hutan	*jungle, forest*		*stop off*

C. Grammar

(147) GIVING ORDERS IN MALAY *(cont.)*

(a) *Marilah kita* corresponds to the rather friendly English form "come on, let's do such and such". See the examples in Section A above.

(b) Probably the easiest and neatest way of giving a polite command in Malay is to ask if the person is able to do something instead of telling him baldly to do it. *Boléh* used in this way is more or less equivalent to the English "please".

(c) *Tak payah,* "there is no need to", is a good way of politely telling or asking someone not to do something. Once again see the examples in Section A above.

(148) JANGAN TIDAK

In Malay, as in English, double negatives cancel each other out quite mathematically. *Jangan tidak,* therefore, does not mean *don't* but *do,* and a very emphatic *do* indeed. It corresponds more or less to "don't fail to" in English.

(149) JANGAN SEKALI-KALI

This is more or less the opposite, or rather the negative, of *jangan tidak.* The English examples in Section A will make this clear. *Kali* really means *time* (in the sense of *occasion*); *sekali* means *once;* so *jangan sekali-kali* (the reduplication is for emphasis) means "don't even once" or "don't ever".

Kali is a useful word:

      sekali   *once*

dua kali	*twice*
tiga kali	*three times, etc.*

Eleventh Week

Minggu Yang Kesebelas

LESSON 53: WEDNESDAY

Pelajaran Yang Ke-53: Hari Rabu

A. Sentences

Saya pun nak pergi juga.	*I'm going too.*
Saya nak baca buku ini; dia pun nak baca juga.	*I'm going to read this book; and he's going to read it too.*
Bésok dia nak pergi ke Raub; lusa saya pun nak pergi juga.	*Tomorrow he's going to Raub; the day after tomorrow I'm going too.*
Bésok dia nak pergi ke Raub; saya pun nak pergi sama.	*Tomorrow he's going to Raub, and I'm going too (i.e. I'm going with him).*
Dia nak makan nasi; saya pun nak makan nasi juga.	*He's going to eat; and I'm going to eat too.*
Dia nak makan nasi; saya pun nak makan nasi sama.	*He's going to eat, and I'm going to eat with him.*
Buku ini saya nak baca; buku itu pun saya nak baca juga.	*I'm going to read this book; and I'm going to read that book too.*

Makanan orang putih
saya tak suka
makan; makanan India
pun saya tak suka
makan juga.

*I don't like European food;
and I don't like
Indian food either.*

Gambar itu saya sudah
téngok; gambar ini
pun saya sudah
téngok juga.

*I have seen that film; I've
also seen this one.*

Saya sudah nampak orang
itu; orang ini pun
saya sudah nampak
juga.

*I have seen that man; this
man I have seen too.*

Hari ini saya nak
pergi ke sana; bésok
pun nak pergi
juga.

*I'm going there today; and
I'm also going there to-
morrow.*

Kerja ini boléh buat
bésok; lusa pun
boléh juga.

*You can do this job to-
morrow; or the day
after tomorrow would be all
right too.*

Boléh buat macam ini;
macam itu pun
boléh juga.

*You can do it this way,
and you can do it
that way too.*

Boléh pergi ikut ini;
ikut itu pun
boléh pergi juga.

*You can go this way, and
you can go that way
too.*

Jangan buat macam ini;
macam itu pun
jangan buat juga.

*Don't do it like this; and
don't do it like that
either.*

Makanan Melayu sangat
sedap; makanan Cina
pun sedap juga.

*Malay food is very tasty;
Chinese food is tasty
too.*

Orang ini orang Cina;
orang itu pun
orang Cina juga.

*This man's a Chinese; so is
that one.*

Bapa saya nak datang
  bésok; emak saya
  pun nak datang
  sama.

*My father's coming tomorrow,
  and my mother's coming
  with him.*

B. Word List

pun...juga	*also, too*	macam ini	*like this, this way*
macam itu	*like that, that way*	ikut ini	*this way (direction)*
ikut itu	*that way (direction)*		

C. Grammar

(150) SAYA PUN NAK PERGI JUGA

Pun followed by *juga* expresses the English *also* or *too*, or, in a negative sentence, *either*. The *pun* is attached to the word referred to by the *also*, the whole group then being placed at the head of the sentence. The word to which *pun* is attached may be almost any part of speech; most commonly it is attached to the subject or object of a sentence or to an adverbial phrase. The *juga* is placed right at the end. The examples in Section A should be carefully studied as they should make this point clear.

(151) JUGA/SAMA

Notice the difference in meaning between such sentences as:

Saya pun nak pergi juga. *I'm also going (i.e. I am going to the same place but not with the other person mentioned.)*

and:

Saya pun nak pergi sama. *I'm going too (i.e. I am going with the other person mentioned).*

Eleventh Week

Minggu Yang Kesebelas

A. Sentences

Apa encik buat?	*What are you doing?*
Saya cuba nak buka kotak besar ini; kotak itu pun kena buka juga.	*I'm trying to open this big box; I've got to open that one too.*
Boléhkah saya tolong encik?	*Can I help you?*
Boléhlah. Sangat susah nak buka kotak dua buah ini.	*Yes, please. These two boxes are difficult to open.*
Saya ingat, baik encik jangan buka macam itu.	*I don't think you should open them like that.*
Macam itu boléh juga; tetapi baik buka macam in.	*I suppose you could do it that way, but it'd be better to open them this way.*
Saya ingat, macam ini pun boléh juga. Boléhkah?	*I think we could do it this way too, couldn't we?*
Boléhlah! Macam itu pun boléh buka juga.	*Yes, of course. We could open them that way too.*
Apa ada dalam kotak ini? Barang encikkah?	*What's in these boxes? Your luggage?*
Barang saya. Saya baharu balik dari England. Saya bercuti di sana.	*Yes. I've just come back from England. I was on leave there.*
Baiklah, kotak ini sudah terbuka sekarang.	*Good. This box is open now.*

Wah! Air sudah masuk ke dalam kotak. Barang saya sudah basah.	*Oh, dear! The water has got into the box. My things are wet.*
Ke dalam kotak ini pun air sudah masuk juga.	*The water's got into this box as well.*
Kotak itu tak apa. Pakaian saya sahaja ada di dalam kotak itu.	*That box doesn't matter. That one's only got my clothes in.*
Pakaian boléh cuci. Dalam kotak ini ada buku saya; buku tak boléh cuci.	*Clothes can be washed. In this box are my books and I can't wash those.*
Saya sudah marah sungguh. Barang ini saya sudah simpan di tempat kering. Orang sudah alih.	*I'm very angry. I put these things away in a dry place. Somebody's moved them.*
Bila saya nak pergi ke England, saya kata kepada orang di sini jangan sekali-kali alih barang saya dari tempat kering itu.	*When I was just off to England, I told the people here not to move my things on any account from the dry place.*
Sekarang barang saya sudah habis basah; apa-apa pun tak boléh buat.	*Now my things are completely soaked, and I can't do anything about it.*
Bila saya pergi ke England nak bercuti, barang saya pun basah juga.	*When I went to England on leave my things got wet as well.*

Saya pun marah juga. Apa-apa pun tak boléh buat.	*I was angry too. There wasn't anything I could do about it.*
Lain kali saya nak simpan di rumah seorang kawan.	*Next time, I shall store them in a friend's house.*
Saya pun nak buat macam itu juga.	*I'll do the same.*

B. Word List

tolong	*help* (vb.)	susah	*difficult*
terbuka	*open* (adj.)	sungguh	*real, really,*
alih	*move* (tr.)		*very true*
lain kali	*next time, another time*	lain	*different*

C. Grammar

(152) PAKAIAN BOLEH CUCI

This sentence defies analysis in terms of English grammar. It is a good example of the absence in Malay of both active and passive voices. Literally, "clothes can clean", you can translate it how you like; here the English passive seems most appropriate: "clothes can be cleaned", but one might argue that the subject has been left out (if that really means anything!) and that "clothes, (you) can clean (them)" would be more correct. However one analyses it, the fact remains that the Malay sentence says, "clothes can clean", and the best thing to do is to get used to that idea. Such sentences are not only possible but common in Malay, although they are impossible in English.

Eleventh Week

Minggu Yang Kèsèbelas

A. Sentences

Masa encik duduk di Malaysia, selalu bercakap Melayu.

When you are living in Malaysia, always speak Malay.

Pergi ke sekolah tiap-tiap hari pada pukul tujuh setengah pagi.

Go to school every day at half past seven in the morning.

Jangan balik sebelum pukul dua petang.

Don't come back before two o'clock in the afternoon.

Jangan bèkerja macam itu; selalu berkerja macam ini.

Don't work like that; always work like this.

Janganlah pergi lagi; bapa saya mahu bèrcakap dengan encik.

Don't go yet; my father would like to speak to you.

Pergilah sekarang téngok apa dia buat.

Please go now and see what he is doing.

Bolèh tuang teh sekarang? Sekejap lagi saya nak keluar.

Would you mind making the tea now? I'm going out in a minute.

Bolèh cuci kerèta saya hari ini? Bèsok saya nak keluar.

Would you clean my car to-day, please? I'm going out tomorrow.

Masa encik bercuti di Negeri Perlis, jangan tidak pergi téngok Pulau Langkawi.

While you're on leave in Perlis, don't miss going to see the island of Langkawi.

Masa encik bercuti di Negeri China, jangan tidak bercakap bahasa Cina.

While you're on leave in China, make sure you speak Chinese.

Jangan sekali-kali pergi
ke kedai makan itu;
makanannya tak
sedap.

*Whatever you do, don't go
to that restaurant; the
food's no good.*

Jangan sekali-kali pergi
téngok wayang
gambar itu.

*On no account go and see
that film.*

Bésok bapa saya nak
datang; lusa emak
saya pun nak
datang juga.

*Tomorrow my father's com-
ing; the day after my
mother's coming, too.*

Bésok dia nak pergi
ke Kuala Lumpur;
lusa pun dià
nak pergi juga.

*Tomorrow he's going to
Kuala Lumpur and the
day after he's going
again.*

Buah durian saya suka
makan; buah
manggis pun saya suka
makan juga.

*I like durians and I also
like mangosteens.*

B. Word List

sebelum	*before (time)*	Negeri China	*China*
Negeri Perlis	*Perlis*		

C. Grammar

(153) Revise the grammar of Lessons 51–54.

Eleventh Week   REVISION LESSON K: WEEK-END

Minggu Yang Kesebelas   Pelajaran Ulangkaji K: Hari Sabtu dan Hari
        Ahad

A. Sentences

Revise all the sentences of Lessons 51–55.

B. Word List

Revise all the word lists of Lessons 51–55.

C. Grammar

Revise all the grammar sections (146–152) of Lessons
51–54.

D. Exercises

(1) Make up thirty sentences using what you have learnt.

(2) Read aloud the following conversations:

A. Apa khabar?

B. Khabar baik. Encik nak ke mana?

A. Saya nak ke stesen kerétapi. Bapa saya nak
sampai dari Ipoh. Dua tiga hari lagi, emak saya pun
nak sampai juga.

B. Emak encik tidak sampai dengan bapa?

A. Tidak. Emak saya ada banyak kerja di sekolah,
tak boléh datang sama.

B. Di mana sekolah emak encik?

A. Sekolah itu di Ipoh. Emak saya guru besar sekolah
itu.

B. Emak saya pun guru besar juga. Sekolah dia di
Bukit Mertajam. Bapa encik tak mahu nanti di
Ipoh sampai emak boléh datang?

A. Mahu juga. Tetapi emak saya kata kepada dia:
Sudah lama anak kita tak téngok bapa; jangan
sekali-kali nantikan saya. Pergilah sekarang.
Sekejap lagi saya pun boléh pergi juga.

B. Sekarang sudah pukul lapan. Pukul lapan sepuluh minit keretapi nak sampai. Baik encik jangan lengah di sini. Pergilah sekarang. Jangan sekali-kali bagi bapa nantikan encik.

(3) Translate the conversation in (2) into English.

(4) Translate into Malay:

(a) My son wants to eat that durian, and your son wants to eat it too.

(b) My father is going to the pictures and my mother is going with him; tomorrow I'm going too.

(c) Whatever you do, don't help that boy; although he is clever, he doesn't want to work.

(d) Don't fail to see the film of "Hang Tuah"; it is a good film.

(e) Would you mind driving my car? My hands (tangan) are sore and I can't drive myself.

(f) Do come to our house: we're having a dinner party tonight.

(g) The railway station at Alor Star is small, and so is the station at Kangar in Perlis.

(h) Don't bother to clean the car today; I'm on holiday tomorrow.

(i) I have been to Singapore twice.

(j) He can also speak Chinese.

A. Sentences

Pasal apa orang itu mahu pergi ke pekan?
Why does that man want to go to town?

Kerana dia mahu beli barang.
Because he wants to do some shopping.

Sebab dia mahu beli barang.
Because he wants to do some shopping.

Pasal apa encik tidak beli keréta baharu?
Why don't you buy a new car?

Kerana duit saya tak cukup.
Because I haven't got enough money.

Pasal apa encik tak mahu belajar bahasa Cina?
Why don't you want to learn Chinese?

Sebab saya tak berapa pandai belajar bahasa asing.
Because I'm not very good at learning foreign languages.

Pasal apa bapa encik sudah masuk hospital?
Why has your father gone into hospital?

Kerana dia sakit dalam perut.
Because he's got stomach trouble.

Pasal apa isteri encik tak beli ikan itu?
Why didn't your wife buy that fish?

Sebab ikan itu mahal sungguh; kita tak tahan belanja.
Because it was very dear, and we couldn't afford it.

Pasal apa orang Cina itu pandai bercakap bahasa Melayu?
Why is that Chinese so good at speaking Malay?

Kerana dia duduk lama di Malaysia— lebih kurang dua puluh tahun.

Because he has been living in Malaysia for a long time — about twenty years.

Encik tahukah pasal apa budak itu tak lulus dalam peperiksaan?

Do you know why that boy did not pass the examination?

Saya ingat dia tak lulus kerana dia tak berapa rajin.

I think he didn't pass because he wasn't very hardworking.

Bapa dia pun semacam juga.

His father's just the same.

Bapa dia sangat malas.

His father is very lazy.

Saya tak tahu pasal apa emak saya belum sampai dari Kuantan.

I don't know why my mother hasn't yet arrived from Kuantan.

Barangkali kerana dia ada banyak kerja di rumah.

Perhaps it's because she has got a lot of work at home.

Dia kena balik berjalan kaki sebab dia tak ada duit lagi.

He had to walk home because he hadn't got any money left.

Tuan saya sangat marah kerana saya lambat sampai ke pejabat.

My boss was very angry because I was late getting to the office.

Saya tak tahu pasal apa dia tak datang lagi; anak saya pun tak tahu juga.

I didn't know why he hadn't yet arrived; and my son didn't know either.

Pasal apa encik tidak datang ke rumah saya malam semalam?

Why didn't you come to my house last night?

Sebab saya demam; saya kena tidur.

Because I got fever; I had to go to bed.

B. Word List

pasal	*concerning, about*	pasal apa	*why*
		kerana	*because*
sebab	*cause, motive; because*	asing	*separate; foreign*
tak berapa	*not very*	rajin	*diligent; hardworking*
perut	*stomach*		
semacam	*the same*	barangkali	*perhaps*
malas	*lazy*	demam	*fever; have a fever*
malam			
semalam	*last night*		

C. Grammar

(154) WHY? and BECAUSE

There are numerous words for *why* and *because* in Malay, but *pasal apa* and *kerana* or *sebab* are the most common in the colloquial language. *Kerana* and *sebab* are interchangeable. From the examples given in Section A it will be obvious that these words are used in just the same way as their English counterparts.

Twelfth Week	LESSON 57: TUESDAY
Minggu Yang Kedua belas	Pelajaran Yang Ke-57: Hari Selasa

A. Sentences

Bila bapa encik nak sampai?	*When will your father arrive?*
Dia nak sampai ésok pada pukul sepuluh pagi.	*He's arriving at ten o'clock tomorrow morning.*

Bila encik datang ke Malaysia?

When did you come to Malaysia?

Saya datang pada tahun seribu sembilan ratus tujuh puluh empat.

I came in 1974.

Bila encik nak balik ke England nak bercuti?

When are you going back to England on leave?

Saya nak pergi ke England tahun depan nak bercuti enam bulan.

I'm going to England next year for six months' leave.

Bila Malaya dapat kemerdekaan?

When did Malaya get her independence?

Malaya sudah merdéka pada bulan Ogos tahun seribu sembilan ratus lima puluh tujuh.

Malay became independent in August 1957.

Bila encik nak bayar hutang encik?

When are you going to pay your debts?

Saya nak bayar hutang saya pada akhir bulan.

I'll pay my debts at the end of the month.

Bila encik dapat gaji?
Biasanya saya dapat gaji pada akhir bulan.

When do you get your salary?
Usually I get my salary at the end of the month.

Pasal apa encik tak minta gaji tiap-tiap minggu?

Why don't you ask for your salary every week?

Sudah minta; tuan saya tak beri juga; dia lagi suka bayar gaji pekerja dia pada akhir bulan.	*I did; but my boss wouldn't give it; he prefers to pay his employees' wages at the end of the month.*
Pasal apa?	*Why?*
Dia kata, sebab macam itu senang lagi.	*He says because it's easier that way.*
Bukan senang; susah. Macam itu orang selalu berhutang.	*It's not easy, it's difficult; in that way people are always in debt.*
Saya bersetuju; macam itu saya tak boléh simpan duit.	*I agree; in that way I can't save any money.*
Pasal apa encik mahu simpan duit?	*Why do you want to save money?*
Sebab saya bukan orang kerajaan; tuan saya tak bagi pencen.	*Because I'm not a government servant; my boss doesn't give a pension.*
Baik encik dapat gaji tiap-tiap minggu; simpan duit dalam Pejabat Pos.	*You'd better get your pay every week and save some money in the post office.*
Saya bersetuju; saya nak minta sekali lagi.	*I agree; I'll ask him again for it.*

B. Word List

bayar	*pay* (vb.)	hutang	*debt*
akhir	*end*	gaji	*salary,*
biasanya	*usually*		*wages, pay*
senang	*easy*	minta	*ask for, demand*

bersetuju	*agree*	berhutang	*indebted, be*
pencen	*pension*		*in debt*
sekali	*again, once*	simpan	
lagi	*more*	duit	*save money*
		kerajaan	*government*
		pekerja	*worker,*
			employee
		orang	*government*
		kerajaan	*servant*

C. Grammar

(155) There is nothing in the sentences in Section A of this lesson which is not self-explanatory.

Twelfth Week	LESSON 58: WEDNESDAY
Minggu Yang Kedua belas	Pelajaran Yang Ke-58; Hari Rabu

A. Sentences

Orang yang saya téngok di pekan—orang Cina.	*The man whom I saw in town was a Chinese.*
Orang yang beri saya buku ini 'nak datang sekali lagi minggu depan.	*The man who gave me this book is coming again next week.*
Budak yang lulus dalam peperiksaan—budak India.	*The boy who passed the examination. is an Indian boy.*
Adakah encik téngok orang Cina yang datang semalam ke rumah kami?	*Did you see the Chinese who came to our house yesterday?*

Di mana buku yang saya
bubuh atas meja
di dalam bilik
encik?

*Where is the book which
I put on the table
in your room?*

Di dalam surat yang
saya dapat sĕmalam
bapa saya kata
dia nak sampai
hari ini.

*In this letter which I
received yesterday my
father says he will
arrive today.*

Orang yang datang ésok
pada pukul enam
ke rumah saya itu
orang Melayu.

*The man who is coming to
my house at six o'clock
tomorrow is a Malay.*

Nama kampung yang
terbakar pada
akhir bulan lepas
itu Kampung
Bahagia.

*The name of the village
which was burned down
at the end of last
month is Kampung
Bahagia.*

Tahun yang saya sam-
pai ke Malaya
itu tahun seribu sem-
bilan ratus lima puluh.

*The year in which I arrived
in Malaya was 1950.*

Yang besar itu saya
tak mahu; yang
kecil pun tak
mahu juga.

*That big one I don't want;
I don't want the
small one either.*

Saya mahu baca buku
itu; boléh encik
beri kepada saya?

*I want to read that book;
please give it to me.*

Yang mana? Yang
mérahkah, yang
hijaukah?

*Which one? The red one
or the green one?*

Yang mérah saya tak mahu; yang hijau pun tak mahu juga. Beri saya yang biru.	*I don't want the red one, and I don't want the green one either. Give me the blue one.*
Yang inikah?	*This one?*
Ya. Yang itu.	*Yes, that one.*
Tetapi yang ini bukan biru; yang ini hijau.	*But this one isn't blue; this one is green.*
Di mana yang murah? Yang ini mahal. Yang murah tak adakah?	*Where are the cheap ones? These (ones) are dear; haven't you got any cheap ones?*

B. Word List

yang	*who, whom, which, that* (rel.)	merah	*red*
		hijau	*green*
biru	*blue*		

C. Grammar

(156) YANG as a relative pronoun

Yang, which we have already had as an indicator of ordinal numerals as well as in a number of set expressions, is used more or less like the English relative pronouns *who, whom, which, that.* It may be the subject or object of the clause it introduces:

orang. yang datang	*the man who comes* (subj.)
orang yang saya nampak	*the man whom I saw* (obj.)

Yang is never used in conjunction with a preposition. If the English sentence would lead one to expect a preposition in the Malay, the preposition is either left out, or the problem is settled by phrasing the sentence differently in Malay:

tahun yang saya sampai ke Malaysia.

the year (in) which I arrived in Malaysia
[In this case notice that we can also say in English: the
year I arrived in Malaysia. I.e. we can leave out both
the preposition and the pronoun.]
méja tempat saya bubuh buku itu
the table on which I put the book
[*tempat*, "place", is used as a kind of relative word
indicating spatial relationship].

(157) YANG...ITU

When the clause introduced by *yang* is very long, there is
a definite danger with the looseness of Malay sentence
structure that we may forget that we are in the middle of a
relative clause and that we may end up by getting
irretrievably lost in the sentence. Therefore, when the
relative clause is getting too long for comfort, Malay
reminds us of what is going on by, as it were, tying the
loose ends together with the word *itu,* which is placed at the
end of the clause. The relative clause then stands within
verbal "brackets", the bracketing words being *yang,* at the
beginning, and *itu,* at the end.

This *itu* refers, not to the word immediately before it,
but to the whole clause which it ends. If the clause would
end in *itu* or *ini,* anyway, then there is no need to add a
second *itu.* Study carefully the second batch of examples in
Section A.

(158) YANG plus ADJECTIVE

When *yang* is used alone with an adjective the effect is
the same as using THE...ONE in English. *Besar* means
"big", but *yang besar* means "the big one". Similarly *yang
mana, yang itu* and *yang ini* mean "which one", "that one"
and "this one" respectively. Look carefully at the third
batch of examples in Section A.

(159) Omission of YANG

In English we can omit the relative pronoun in speaking

except when it is the subject of its clause. For instance, although we cannot omit the *who* in "the man who came", we can omit the pronoun in "the man (whom) I saw" or "the book (which) I read it in".

In Malay, too, *yang* is often omitted where it can be in English, and also even when it is the subject provided that no ambiguity results. Examples:

buku saya baca	*the book I read*
rumah kita duduk	*the house we live in*

For the time being, however, until the student has a greater feeling for the language, it would be better not to omit *yang,* as the dangers of ambiguity are great.

Yang, can, of course never be omitted in the adjectival construction described in (158).

Twelfth Week	LESSON 59: THURSDAY
Minggu Yang Kedua belas	Pelajaran Yang ke 59: Hari Khamis

A. Sentences

Rumah besar.	*A big house.*
Rumah yang besar.	*A big house.*
Dia sudah beli sebuah rumah besar.	*He's bought a big house.*
Dia sudah beli rumah yang besar.	*He's bought a big house.*
Saya sudah jual keréta yang kecil; saya nak beli yang besar.	*I've sold the small car; I'm going to buy a big one.*
Orang yang bodoh tak suka bekerja kuat.	*Stupid people don't like working hard.*

Orang yang sakit pun
tak suka bekerja
kuat juga.

*Sick people don't like
working hard either.*

Orang ini sudah ·sakit;
bawa dia ke
hospital baharu.

*This man's been taken ill;
take him to the
new hospital.*

Saya sangat suka
makan makanan
Cina yang sedap.

*I'm very fond of tasty
Chinese food.*

Orang Cina yang
gemuk ini bapa
budak Cina yang
kurus itu.

*This fat Chinese is the
father of that thin
Chinese boy.*

Keréta baharu yang
besar itu keréta
bapa saya.

*That big new car is my
father's.*

Buku hijau yang kecil
ini buku emak
dia.

*This small green book is his
mother's.*

Orang tua yang gemuk
itu emak budak
muda yang kurus
ini.

*That fat old woman is this
thin young lad's mother.*

Orang yang sangat bodoh
tak tahu bercakap
bahasa sendiri.

*Very stupid people do not
know how to talk
their own language.*

Orang itu orang yang
baik sungguh.

*That man is a really good
fellow.*

Orang yang datang ke-
sekolah kita itu
orang yang sangat
jahat.

*The man who came to our
school is a really wicked
person.*

Buku yang ini buku
yang baik sekali.

*This book is a really ex-
cellent book.*

Budak ini budak yang rajin sekali di dalam sekolah kita.	*This boy is the most industrious boy in our school.*
Keréta ini keréta yang mahal sekali: harganya lima puluh ribu ringgit.	*This car is the most expensive; it costs fifty thousand dollars.*
Buku ini buku yang berguna sekali.	*This book is the most useful one.*

B. Word List

bodoh	*stupid*	gemuk	*fat*
kurus	*thin*	jahat	*wicked*
berguna	*useful*		

C. Grammar

(160) RUMAH BESAR, RUMAH YANG BESAR

The difference between these two phrases is that the *yang* in the second one throws the emphasis on to the adjective. If we say, *dia sudah beli sebuah rumah besar* (he has bought a big house), we are more interested in the house than in its size, whereas when we say, *dia sudah beli rumah yang besar,* we mean that we knew that the man was going to buy a house, and that out of all the houses he might have bought, he's bought a big one. That is, we are more interested in the size than in the house.

(161) MAKANAN CINA YANG SEDAP

When a noun is qualified by more than one adjective, the last one normally has *yang* in front of it.

(162) ORANG YANG SANGAT BODOH

When the adjective qualifying a noun is itself qualified by an adverb, *yang* should be used as well. It could be omitted, but it is better Malay to retain it.

(163) BUDAK YANG RAJIN SEKALI

Note this way of indicating a superlative: YANG plus adjective plus SEKALI.

Twelfth Week

Minggu Yang Kedua belas

LESSON 60: FRIDAY

Pelajaran Yang Ke-60: Hari Jumaat

A. Sentences

Pasal apa orang itu tidak makan daging babi?

Why doesn't that man eat pork?

Dia tidak boléh makan daging babi kerana dia orang Melayu.

He can't eat pork because he's a Malay.

Pasal apa encik sudah datang ke Pulau Pinang?

Why have you come to Penang?

Saya sudah datang ke sini sebab saya mahu téngok bapa saya di hospital.

I have come here because I want to see my father in hospital.

Pasal apa dia tak lulus dalam peperiksaan?

Why didn't he pass the examination?

Dia tak lulus kerana dia tak cukup rajin.

He didn't pass because he didn't work hard enough.

Bila encik nak masuk
sekolah menengah?

*When are you going to
the secondary school?*

Saya nak masuk sekolah
menengah Inggeris
tahun depan.

*I'm going to the English
secondary school
next year.*

Bila encik beli keréta
yang baharu itu?

*When did you buy that
new car?*

Keréta yang baharu
ini saya beli
bulan lepas.

*I bought this new car last
month.*

Orang Cina yang mahu
beli keréta saya
yang lama itu
nak datang lagi
sekali pada pukul lima
setengah.

*The Chinese who wants to
buy my old car is
coming again at half
past five.*

Encik nak jual yang
lamakah? Saya ingat
yang baharu.

*You're going to sell the
old one, are you? I
thought it was the new one.*

Yang baharukah? Tidak!
Saya tak mahu
jual yang baharu.

*The new one? No! I
don't want to sell
the new one.*

Sekolah yang baharu ini
sekolah rendah;
yang lama itu
sekolah menengah.

*This new school is a primary
school; that old one
is a secondary school.*

Bangunan yang besar
sekali itu ialah
sebuah universiti.

*That extremely large build-
ing is a university.*

B. Word List

menengah	*secondary*	rendah	*low; primary*
universiti	*university*		

C. Grammar

(164) Revise the grammar of Lessons 56–59.

Twelfth Week   REVISION LESSON L: WEEK-END

Minggu Yang Kedua belas   Pelajaran Ulangkaji L: Hari Sabtu dan Hari
                                                Ahad

A. Sentences

Revise all the sentences of Lessons 56–60.

B. Word List

Revise all the word lists of Lessons 56–60.

C. Grammar

Revise all the grammar sections (154–164) of Lessons 56–59.

D. Exercises

(1) Make up fifty sentences using what you have learnt during the course.

(2) Read aloud the following conversation:

A. Apa khabar, encik?

B. Khabar baik, encik. Siapa orang yang saya téngok semalam itu di luar rumah encik?

A. Itu bapa saya. Semalam pada pukul empat saya duduk di luar rumah; tiba-tiba bapa saya sampai dari Kuala Lumpur.

B. Encik tak tahukah dia nak datang?

A. Tidak. Saya bertanya kepada bapa, pasal apa dia tak tulis surat beritahu saya pukul berapa dia nak datang.

B. Apa dia kata?

A. Dia kata dia tak boléh beritahu saya, sebab dia tak

tahu sendiri. Dia datang sahaja kerana dia mahu saya téngok keréta yang baharu. Dia beli daripada seorang putih yang nak pergi ke England bercuti. Orang putih itu guru besar sebuah sekolah menengah Inggeris di Negeri Selangor.

B. Berapa lama bapa encik nak tinggal di sini?

A. Saya tak tahu lagi. Bapa saya sudah demam; doktor kata dia kena tidur dua tiga hari. Lepas itu dia boléh balik ke Kuala Lumpur.

B. Boléhkah saya datang ke rumah encik nak téngok bapa encik?

A. Boléhlah. Marilah encik petang ini.

(3) Translate the conversation in (2) into English.

(4) Read aloud the following conversation between Felix, a student of Malay, and Zainal, his munshi:

Z. Apa khabar, Felix?

F. Khabar baik, Cik Zainal.

Z. Boléh Felix kata kepada saya, bila Felix mulai belajar bahasa Melayu?

F. Boléh. Saya mulai belajar bahasa Melayu lebih-kurang tiga bulan dahulu.

Z. Macam mana bahasa Melayu kita? Felix ingat senangkah nak belajar?

F. Bahasa Melayu bukan bahasa senang, bukan bahasa susah. Kalau orang mahu belajar bahasa asing, kena bekerja kuat. Tetapi kalau orang suka bekerja kuat, saya ingat bahasa Melayu senang nak belajar.

Z. Pasal apa encik mahu belajar bahasa Melayu?

F. Sekarang Malaysia sudah merdéka. Bahasa Melayu itu sudah jadi (become) bahasa…er…bahasa…, apa orang Melayu panggil (call) "national language"?

Z. Orang Melayu kata "bahasa kebangsaan".

F. Terima kasih. Bahasa Melayu sudah jadi bahasa kebangsaan kita. Saya ingat semua orang yang duduk
di Malaysia kena belajar bahasa kebangsaan kita.
Orang Melayu pun, orang India pun, orang Cina pun
tak apa. Kita semua mahu jadi orang Malaysia.
Kalau kita tak belajar bahasa Melayu, macam mana
kita nak jadi orang Malaysia?

Z. Saya bersetuju dengan encik. Encik belajar bahasa
Melayu tiga bulan sahaja, tahu bercakap baik
sungguh juga.

F. Saya tak tahu bercakap banyak lagi, tetapi saya
nak belajar lagi. Saya sudah beli buku Melayu nak
baca.

Z. Buku yang mana encik nak baca?

F. Saya nak baca Hikayat Hang Tuah. Buku itu
baikkah?

Z. Baik sungguh.

(5) Translate the conversation in (4) into English.

(6) Translate into Malay:

(a) That school is a secondary school.
(b) Although he is headmaster of a Chinese secondary
school, he can't speak Mandarin (bahasa Mandarin).
(c) That large green car is my father's.
(d) The film we saw last night in town was a very
good Malay picture.
(e) The terrorists who were sentenced to death last
month are now dead. They were hanged in Pudu
Gaol.
(f) Because Malaysia is now independent, we must all
learn Bahasa Malaysia.
(g) Boys are learning Bahasa Malaysia in the
primary schools; they are learning it in the secondary schools too.

(h) Give me that book, please. Which one? The blue one.

(i) Chinese, Malays, Indians—all are Malaysians.

(j) The Europeans are beginning to go home because their work in Malaysia is finished.

(k) Why don't you learn English? Because I am not very good at learning foreign languages.

(l) English and Malay are very useful languages.

(m) What time is it now? It is twenty to eleven.

(n) In what year did Malaya gain her independence? In the year 1957.

(o) I was born (dilahirkan) on the 26th of March 1925.

(p) How many cigarettes are there in that box? There are forty-seven.

(q) How many letters did you receive this morning? I got four.

(r) This boy can't write his own name!

(s) This boy has been taken ill. Take him to the hospital in a trishaw; he can't walk.

(t) The bride whom we saw at the bersanding ceremony last week was very pretty.

THE KEY TO THE TRANSLATION
AND OTHER EXERCISES CONTAINED IN
THE REVISION LESSONS

REVISION LESSON A

Exercise D (2)

In the Market

A. Is this a Malay market?
B. No, it isn't; it's a Chinese market.

A. Is that man a Chinese?
B. Yes, he is.

A. What is he selling?
B. He is selling meat.

A. What meat is he selling?
B. Pork, beef and mutton.

A. Where does he sell that meat?
B. In a shop.

A. What is this man selling in this shop?
B. He is selling book and newspapers.

A. Malay books and newspapers?
B. No. He's a Chinese. He sells Chinese books and newspapers.

Exercise D (3)

(a) Apa dia jual di kedai itu?
(b) Budak perempuan itu orang Cina.
(c) Budak laki-laki ini orang putih.
(d) Budak perempuan India ini makan nasi dan daging kambing.
(e) Di mana kedai itu?
(f) Budak laki-laki Cina itu tulis apa?
(g) Dia tulis surat.
(h) Di mana dia beli daging babi?
(i) Orang perempuan itu orang Melayu.
(j) Orang perempuan Melayu itu beli daging kambing di kedai itu.

REVISION LESSON B

Exercise D (3)

A. Hullo, how are you?

B. I'm fine, thanks.

A. Where is there a Malay restaurant?

B. There's a Malay restaurant in the Malay market.

A. Are there many people in that restaurant (lit. shop; it is unnecessary to repeat the *makan* "ad nauseam" once we have established the fact that the shop is an eating-shop).

B. Yes, there are. There's a lot of Malays in that restaurant.

A. What do they eat?

B. In that restaurant there are people eating rice, there are people eating mutton, and there are people eating beef.

A. What do they drink there?

B. Some drink tea, some drink coffee, and some drink water. (Notice this more idiomatic English way of translating a series of *ada orang*'s.)

A. Is there anybody eating fruit?

B. Yes.

A. What fruit do people eat in that restaurant?

B. Some eat durians, some eat mangosteens, and some eat rambutans.

A. Cheerio!

B. Bye-bye!

Exercise D (4)

(a) Siapa nama encik?

(b) Nama saya Ah Chong. Saya orang Cina.

(c) Encik makan daging babi? Makan.

(d) Encik makan daging lembu? Tidak; saya orang India; orang India tidak makan daging lembu.

(e) Orang Cina itu jual apa?

(f) Dia jual buku dan suratkhabar.

(g) Bapa encik di mana? Bapa saya (ada) di Kuala Lumpur.

(h) Anak encik ada keréta? Tak ada.

(i) Saya ada basikal. Saya tak ada keréta.

(j) Orang Melayu itu ada keréta lembu.

REVISION LESSON C

Exercise D (3)

A. Trishaw! Come here!
B. All right, sir. Where do you want to go to?
A. I want to go to Kuala Lumpur. I want to go to the pictures there.
B. All right, sir. You'd better get in my trishaw.
(Later)
B. O.K., sir. Here is the cinema.
A. Good. Thank you. Good-bye.
B. Good-bye, sir.

Exercise D (4)

(a) Encik mahu naik apa pergi ke Singapura?
(b) Saya mahu naik kerétapi.
(c) Encik tak mahu naik keréta?
(d) Tak mahu. Saya tak suka naik keréta.
(e) Bapa saya balik dari rumah emak saya di Raub hari ini.
(f) Budak Melayu ini mahu belajar bahasa Cina.
(g) Baik dia pergi ke Kuala Lumpur belajar di sana.
(h) Emak saya mulaï belajar bahasa Tamil semalam.
(i) Encik tahu bercakap bahasa Inggeris? Tak tahu.
(j) Semalam saya pergi ke Singapura beli keréta; tak dapat beli.
(k) Tulis surat kepada orang Cina itu.
(l) Hari ini saya terima surat daripada emak saya.
(m) Saya beri buah durian kepada dia hari ini.
(n) Bésok saya dapat surat daripada dia.
(o) Baik kita tulis surat kepada dia.

REVISION LESSON D

Exercise D (3)

A. Where did you go to yesterday?
B. I went to Kuala Lumpur.
A. What did you do in Kuala Lumpur?
B. I went to a Chinese restaurant.
A. What did you eat in that restaurant?
B. I ate rice, pork, and three rambutans.

A. Were there a lot of people in the restaurant yesterday?

B. Yes. There were fourteen Chinese eating there; also*there were two or three** Europeans drinking coffee. There weren't any Malays and Indians yesterday.

A. Did you come back today?

B. Yes, I did. I returned here by train.

A. Didn't you return here by car?

B. No. I haven't got a car. I sold my car yesterday in Kuala Lumpur.

Exercise D (4)

(a) Saya ada tiga BUAH keréta.

(b) Di kedai itu ada lima ORANG Melayu.

(c) Ada empat ORANG penumpang naik keréta itu.

(d) Berapa BIJI durian encik beli di pasar?

(e) Berapa ÉKOR kucing encik ada di rumah encik?

Exercise D (5)

Tiga, tujuh, sembilan, sebelas, empat belas, tujuh belas, lapan belas, dua puluh tiga, dua puluh enam, tiga puluh tiga, empat puluh empat, lima puluh lima, lima puluh tujuh, enam puluh lapan, tujuh puluh tujuh, tujuh puluh sembilan, lapan puluh, lapan puluh empat, lapan puluh enam, sembilan puluh, sembilan puluh tiga, sembilan puluh lima, sembilan puluh sembilan, seratus.

Seratus enam †, seratus tiga puluh tiga, seratus lima puluh empat, seratus enam puluh tujuh, seratus tujuh puluh lapan, seratus lapan puluh lapan, seratus sembilan puluh, seratus sembilan puluh sembilan.

dan lagi: (lit. and more) means *also, furthermore.*

**dua tiga:* (lit. two-three) means *two OR three,* i.e. there is no need to translate the English *or* in such a context in Malay.

†*Seratus enam:* English says one *hundred AND six:* Malay does not use *dan* in such a context.

Exercise D (6)

(a) Berapa orang anak encik ada?

(b) Saya ada dua orang anak laki-laki dan tiga orang anak perempuan.

(c) Bapa saya ada dua buah keréta.

(d) Saya makan tujuh biji manggis semalam.

(e) Orang Melayu itu ada tiga puluh ékor lembu.

(f) Ada lima puluh tiga orang penumpang naik kerétapi itu.

(g) Kapal api itu ada seratus orang penumpang.

(h) Emak saya beli dua puluh empat biji telur di pasar Melayu.

(i) Anak perempuan saya suka makan telur.

(j) Di hospital ini ada seratus lima puluh orang sakit.

REVISION LESSON E

Exercise D (3)

A. Hullo, how are you?

B. I'm fine thanks. Where are you off to?

A. I'm going to go to the market to do some shopping. After that I'm going to a restaurant for a meal.

B. Can I come too?

B. Yes, of course.

B. What are you going to buy in the market?

A. I'm going to buy fish, meat and some durians.

B. But fish is very dear today; you'd better just buy the meat.

A. I didn't know fish was very expensive; my wife said fish was cheap in this town.

B. No, it isn't. Fish here is very expensive.

A. All right. I won't buy any. Where is there a Malay restaurant? I'm very fond of Malay curry.

B. In the Malay market there are two good restaurants. We can go to that restaurant over there. Their curry is first class. I'll come with you and eat there. Do you mind?

A. Of course not. Come on; let's go and eat now. After that we can do the shopping for my wife.

B. Do you like hot curry? In that restaurant the curry is very hot.

A. You bet! The hotter the better.*

B. What shall we drink with the curry?

A. We'd better just drink water.

---

* Note the construction

Exercise D (4)

(i) [Southern way]

Tiga ringgit lima puluh sén; sepuluh ringgit dua puluh lima sén; enam puluh sén; lima puluh enam ringgit tujuh puluh sén; seratus tiga puluh enam ringgit empat puluh lima sén.

(ii) [Northern way]

Tiga ringgit lima kupang; sepuluh ringgit dua kupang lima; enam kupang; lima puluh enam ringgit tujuh kupang; seratus tiga puluh enam ringgit empat kupang lima.

Exercise D (5)

(a) Saya nak ke pasar beli barang; lepas itu saya nak makan nasi di sebuah kedai makan Cina. Encik mahu pergi sama?

(b) Mahulah. Saya sangat suka makan makanan Cina. Makanan baik di kedai makan itu?

(c) Di mana encik beli keréta baharu itu? Saya beli semalam di Singapura. Encik mahu naik?

(d) Semalam saya dapat surat daripada emak saya di Seremban. Dia kata bapa saya ada di hospital di Kuala Lumpur.

(e) Buku ini berapa harganya? Harganya lima belas ringgit. Itu sangat mahal. Bukan mahal; murah. Buku ini sangat baik.

(f) Orang putih itu sangat suka makan gulai Melayu sangat pedas. Dia kata, "Lagi pedas lagi baik."

(g) Saya tak tahu orang putih suka makan gulai. Sukalah. Ramai orang putih suka makan makanan Melayu.

(h) Encik nak pergi ke mana bésok? Saya nak ke Kuala Kangsar téngok bapa saya sakit. Emak saya ingat dia sakit kuat.

(i) Téh ini sangat hangat; saya tak boléh minum.

(j) Gulai ini sangat pedas; dia tak boléh makan.

REVISION LESSON F

Exercise D (3)

A. Hullo, how are you?

B. I'm fine. Where are you off to?

A. I'm off to town.

B. What are you going to do in town?

A. I'm going to buy a new car.

B. But you've got a big car.

A. That car I sold in Ipoh last Saturday.

B. (When) you sold that car, what did you get for it?

A. For that car I got $3,500. That car was very big, I'm going to buy a small car.

A. How much do you want to pay for the new car?

A. I'm thinking of paying about four thousand.

B. Can I come to the town with you? I know where you can buy a good car.

A. Yes, of course. Thanks very much.

B. Afterwards what are you going to do in town?

A. I was thinking of eating in a Chinese restaurant. Are you fond of Chinese food?

B. Yes, I am indeed.

A. You'd better come too; you can eat with me.

B. Thank you very much.

A. Don't mention it.

Exercise D (4)

(a) Semalam saya jual keréta saya di Kuala Lumpur; saya dapat empat ribu lima ratus ringgit.

(b) Bésok saya beli keréta baharu di Singapura.

(c) Semalam hari Sabtu; saya bercuti dua hari; saya pergi ke Batu Feringgi di Pulau Pinang nak berenang.

(d) Seorang kawan saya kata, "Berbahaya sikit nak berenang di Batu Feringgi; ada banyak ular selimpat di sana; baik encik duduk di pantai sahaja."

(e) Orang Melayu suka makan buah pinang, tetapi orang putih tidak suka makan.

(f) Orang Kedah tidak kata, "Saya nak pergi ke Pulau Pinang"; selalu kata, "Saya nak pergi ke Tanjung" [or "Saya nak pi Tanjung"].

(g) Ramai orang Melayu tidak suka makan, makanan Cina; makanan Cina ada banyak daging babi; orang Melayu tak boléh makan daging babi.

(h) Bandar Alor Setar ada lebih kurang lima puluh ribu orang.

(i) Malaya ada lebih kurang enam juta orang.

(j) England ada lebih kurang lima puluh juta orang.

REVISION LESSON G

Exercise D (3)

At ten past twelve at night I arrived at my house. I had a bath and after that I went to bed. This morning I got up a bit late—at a quarter to eight. Straightaway I had my bath, ate some bread and drank some coffee. Then I got into my car to go to the office. At a quarter to nine I arrived there; my boss was very angry. He said: "You are late—a quarter of an hour!" I said, "Sir, last night I went to the house of a friend of mine. His son was getting married. I stayed at his place until twelve o'clock at night to see the bersanding ceremony. I went to bed at one o'clock in the morning, and was a bit late getting up this morning." My boss is a good fellow. He said, "All right! But there's a lot of work today. Could you stay in the office until seven o'clock in the evening?" I replied, "Certainly, sir."

Exercise D (4)

  (a) Anak perempuan saya nak berkahwin hari ini; nak ada kenduri besar di rumah pengantin laki-laki.

  (b) Ramai orang nak pergi ke sana nak téngok istiadat bersanding pada pukul sepuluh setengah.

  (c) Anak saya sangat cantik; pengantin laki-laki sangat suka hati.

  (d) Saya ingat kita nak tidur léwat malam ini.

  (e) Pelajaran ini pelajaran ulangkaji.

  (f) Kapalterbang India itu tiba ke Singapura pada pukul sebelas lima puluh tujuh minit malam.

  (g) Pagi ini saya lambat nak datang ke pejabat; tuan saya sangat marah.

  (h) Tiap-tiap hari dia cuba bercakap Melayu dengan orang Melayu di pejabat; lagi dia cuba, lagi dia pandai bercakap.

  (i) Tuan saya nak pergi ke England bulan depan nak bercuti.

  (j) Saya tak tahu di mana buku saya. Boléh téngok buku encik? Boléhlah.

REVISION LESSON H

Exercise D (2)

  (a) Orang itu orang Cina?
     Adakah orang itu orang Cina?

Orang itu orang Cinakah?

(b) Encik tahu bercakap bahasa Tamil?
Adakah encik tahu bercakap bahasa Tamil?
Encik tahukah bercakap bahasa Tamil?

(c) Bapa diakah nak datang ésok?
Adakah bapa dia nak datang ésok?

(d) Emak encik sudah mati?
Adakah emak encik sudah mati?
Emak encik sudah matikah?

(e) Dia sudah dapat surat daripada bapa dia?
Adakah dia sudah dapat surat daripada bapa dia?
Dia sudah dapat suratkah daripada bapa dia?

Exercise D (4)

A. Hullo, how are you?

B. I'm fine, thanks. How is your father?

A. My father's very fit, but a friend of mine is ill. He's gone into hospital in Kuala Lumpur. He is very ill.

A. I was told that your father is ill; how's he getting on?

B. He's doing very nicely. Last week he was very ill, and went into hospital in Ipoh, but now he's better. He's come out of hospital to go home again. He's bought himself a new car, and now he's going to Singapore for three weeks' holiday there.

A. Good show! Where is he staying in Singapore?

B. He's going to stay with a friend of mine.

A. Is he an Indian?

B. No. My friend is a European. He has a house on the beach; my father will be able to rest on the beach and look at the sea.

A. Will he go swimming?

B. My father? No, he won't. He can't swim.

Exercise D (5)

(a) Adakah emak encik tahu berenang? Tak.

(b) Orang India itu tahukah bercakap bahasa Inggeris? Tak tahu. Dia tahu bercakap bahasa Tamil sahaja.

(c) Bapa Encik Ahmad sudah mati.

(d) Bapa encik sudahkah beli rumah besar itu di Ipoh? Belum.

(e) Mula-mula dia tak tahu bercakap Melayu, tetapi tahun lepas tiap-tiap hari dia pergi ke sekolah hendak belajar. Sekarang dia sudah sangat pandai bercakap Melayu.

(f) Sudah lama orang Cina itu duduk di Malaysia tetapi dia tidak pandai bercakap Melayu.

(g) Sekarang Malaysia sudah merdéka.

(h) Gibraltar belum merdéka.

(i) Sudah tiga tahun saya belajar bahasa Cina, tetapi saya belum pandai bercakap lagi.

(j) Adakah encik suka duduk di pantai nak téngok laut? Ya suka.

REVISION LESSON I

Exercise D (3)

A. Have you read the paper today?

B. Yes. I read that two bandits have been shot in Selangor, and two more have been captured.

A. What will happen to the other two?

B. I don't know yet. I should think they'll be sentenced to death. They are not young men.

A. Was there anything else in the newspaper today?

B. Oh, yes. A village has been burned down. A hundred people were injured. A lot of people are in hospital.

A. Where was the village?

B. I've forgotten. I think it was somewhere in Kelantan.

A. What a shame for the villagers!—What else was there in the newspaper?

B. I read that a friend of mine in Ipoh got married yesterday. Her bersanding ceremony was very fine. There's nothing else today.

Exercise D (4)

(a) Orang tua itu sudah kena denda dua ratus ringgit. Kasihan dia!
(b) Encik ada apa-apa kena cukai?
(c) Tak ada. Barang ini satu pun tak kena cukai.
(d) Bapa dia sudah mati kena langgar keréta.
(e) Lima orang penjahat sudah kena hukum gantung; tiga orang lagi sudah kena hukum penjara.
(f) Semalam di Negeri Selangor seorang pengganas pun tak kena tangkap.
(g) Buku itu di mana-mana pun saya tak boléh beli.
(h) Buah durian ini sebiji pun tak sedap.
(i) Di kampung ini seorang pun tidak tahu bercakap Melayu.
(j) Dalam kotak itu apa pun tak ada.
(k) Dalam kotak ini ada lima puluh batang rokok.
(l) Sebatang rokok pun saya tak ada lagi.
(m) Hari ini surat sepucuk pun dia belum terima.
(n) Siapa pun tak ada dalam bilik saya.
(o) Hidung dia sudah luka kena pisau cukur.

REVISION LESSON J

Exercise D (3)

A. Have you been ill? You didn't come to the office yesterday?
B. Yes, I was rather poorly. Yesterday I was walking along the side of the road, when suddenly a big car came along; I didn't see it and fell into the drain.
A. There was a lot of water in the drains yesterday. Did you get your clothes wet?
B. Yes, I did. But my body was not harmed, however. But the doctor said I'd better stay at home in bed yesterday. I didn't want to come to the office.

Exercise D (4)

(a) Orang itu orang India, pandai bercakap bahasa Cina juga.

(b) Budak Cina ini tak suka makan daging babi pula!

(c) Tikus lari ke dalam lobang dia di bawah almari, kucing tangkap juga.

(d) Encik suka makan makanan Inggeris? Suka juga; tetapi saya lagi suka makan makanan Melayu.

(e) Encik mahukah pergi téngok wayang gambar? Mahulah! Sudah lama saya tak pergi téngok wayang gambar. Terima kasih.

(f) Saya sudah bubuh lima puluh batang rokok ke dalam kotak ini. Encik mahu hisapkah?

(g) Bapa saya sudah sangat tua; dia tak suka téngok orang perempuan hisap rokok.

(h) Emak dia orang tua, dia hisap lima puluh batang rokok sehari pula!

(i) Gulai Melayu sangat pedas, ramai orang putih suka makan juga.

(j) Gulai itu pedaskah? Pedas juga.

REVISION LESSON K

Exercise D (3)

A. Hullo!

B. Hullo! Where are you off to?

A. I'm going to the railway station. My father is arriving from Ipoh. In two or three days, my mother will be coming too.

B. Isn't your mother arriving with your father?

A. No. My mother has a lot of work at school, and she can't come with him.

B. Where is your mother's school?

A. It's in Ipoh. My mother is the headmistress of the school.

B. My mother is a headmistress too. Her school is at Bukit Mertajam. Doesn't your father want to wait in Ipoh until your mother can come?

A. Well, yes, he did want to. But my mother said to him, "Our son hasn't seen his father for a long time; for goodness' sake don't wait for me. Go now, and I'll soon be able to go too."

B. It's now eight o'clock. The train's arriving at ten past eight. You'd

better not hang about here. Whatever you do, don't keep your
father waiting for you.

Exercise D (4)

(a) Anak saya mahu makan buah durian itu; anak encik pun mahu
makan juga.

(b) Bapa saya nak pergi téngok wayang gambar; emak pun nak pergi
sama. Ésok saya pun nak pergi juga.

(c) Jangan sekali-kali tolong budak itu; dia pandai, tak mahu bekerja
juga.

(d) Jangan tidak pergi téngok gambar "Hang Tuah"; gambar itu
gambar baik.

(e) Boléhkah encik bawa keréta saya? Tangan saya sakit; tak boléh
bawa sendiri.

(f) Marilah ke rumah kami nak ada jamuan makan malam ini.

(g) Stesen kerétapi di Alor Setar kecil; stesen di Kangar di Negeri Perlis
pun kecil juga.

(h) Tak payah cuci keréta hari ini; ésok saya nak bercuti.

(i) Dua kali saya sudah pergi ke Singapura.

(j) Bahasa cina pun dia tahu cakap juga.

REVISION LESSON L

Exercise D (3)

A. Hullo, how are you?

B. I'm fine, thanks. How are you? Who was that man I saw yesterday outside your house?

A. That was my father. At four o'clock yesterday I was sitting outside the house, when suddenly my father arrived from Kuala
Lumpur.

b. Didn't you know he was coming?

A. No. I asked my father why he didn't write a letter to let me know
what time he was coming.

B. What did he say?

A. He said he couldn't let me know, because he didn't know himself. He only came because he wanted me to see the new car. He
bought it from a European who was going to England on leave.

The European was the headmaster of an English secondary school in Selangor.

B. How long is your father staying here?

A. I don't know yet. My father has caught a fever, and the doctor says he must stay in bed for two or three days. After that he can go back to Kuala Lumpur.

B. Can I come to your house and see your father?

A. Of course. Come this afternoon.

Exercise D (5)

Z. Hullo, Felix!

F. Hullo, Zainal!

Z. Can you tell me, Felix, when you began learning Malay?

F. Yes. I began to learn Malay about three months ago.

Z. How do you find this Malay language of ours? Do you think it's easy to learn, Felix?

F. Malay is neither easy nor difficult. If you want to learn a foreign language, you have to work hard. But if you like working hard, I think Malay is easy to learn.

Z. Why do you want to learn Malay?

F. Malaysia is now independent. Malay has become our ... er ... our ..., what do the Malays say for "national language"?

Z. The Malays say, "bahasa kebangsaan".

F. Thank you. Malay has become our national language. I think that everybody who lives in Malaysia should learn our national language. Malays, Indians, or Chinese, it doesn't matter. We all want to be Malaysians. If we don't learn Malay, how are we going to become Malaysians?

Z. I agree with you. Although you have been studying Malay for only three months, you can speak it really well.

F. I can't talk much yet, but I'm going to go on learning. I've bought a Malay book to read.

Z. Which book are you going to read?

F. I'm going to read the Hikayat Hang Tuah. Is that a good book?

Z. Yes, very good.

Exercise D (6)

(a) Sekolah itu sekolah menengah.

(b) Dia guru besar sebuah sekolah menengah Cina, dia tak tahu ber cakap bahasa Mandarin pula!

(c) Keréta hijau yang besar itu keréta bapa saya.

(d) Gambar yang kita téngok malam semalam di pekan itu gambar Melayu yang sangat baik.

(e) Pengganas yang kena hukum gantung bulan lepas itu, sudah mati sekarang. Orang itu kena gantung di Penjara Pudu.

(f) Kerana sekarang Malaysia sudah merdéka, kita semua kena belajar bahasa kebangsaan.

(g) Budak laki-laki belajar bahasa kebangsaan di sekolah rendah; di sekolah menengah pun belajar juga.

(h) Boléh beri saya buku itu. Yang mana? Yang biru.

(i) Orang Cina, orang Melayu, orang India, semua orang Malaysia.

(j) Orang putih mulaï nak balik sebab kerja orang putih di Malaysia sudah habis.

(k) Pasal apa encik tidak belajar bahasa Inggeris? Kerana saya tak berapa pandai nak belajar bahasa asing.

(l) Bahasa Inggeris dan bahasa Melayu bahasa yang berguna sungguh.

(m) Pukul berapa sekarang? Sudah pukul sepuluh empat puluh minit.

(n) Pada tahun berapa Malaya dapat kemerdekaan? Pada tahun seribu sembilan   ratus lima puluh tujuh.

(o) Saya dilahirkan pada dua puluh enam haribulan Mac tahun seribu sembilan ratus dua puluh lima.

(p) Berapa batang rokok ada di dalam kotak itu? Ada empat puluh tujuh batang.

(q) Berapa pucuk surat encik terima pagi tadi?

(r) Budak ini tak tahu tulis nama sendiri.

(s) Budak ini sudah sakit. Bawa dia naik béca pergi ke hospital. Dia tak boléh berjalan kaki.

(t) Pengantin perempuan yang kita téngok di istiadat bersanding minggu lepas itu, cantik sungguh.

CLASSIFIERS

The following is a list of the most common classifiers with examples of their use.

(1) BATANG *(stem)*
This classifier is used with long stick-like objects. Examples:

sebatang rokok	*a cigarette*
sebatang tongkat	*a walking-stick*
sebatang jari	*a finger*

(2) BENTUK *(curve)*
This classifier is used for ring- and hook-shaped objects. Examples:

sebentuk kail	*a fish-hook*
sebentuk cincin	*a ring*

(3) BIDANG *(broad)*
This classifier is used with hides, sails, mats and land. Examples:

sebidang kajang	*a palm leaf mat*
sebidang tanah	*a stretch of land*

(4) BIJI *(seed)*
This classifier is very common and is used of almost any small object. Examples:

sebiji telur	*an egg*
sebiji durian	*a durian*
sebiji cawan	*a cup*

(5) BILAH *(narrow strip)*
This classifier is quite common and is used with sharp or knife-like objects. Examples:

sebilah pisau	*a knife*
sebilah pedang	*a sword*
sebilah gigi	*a tooth*

(6) BUAH *(fruit)*

This is one of the commonest classifiers, being used with almost any large inanimate object. Examples:

sebuah buku	*a book*
sebuah kapal	*a ship*
sebuah keréta	*a car*
sebuah kerusi	*a chair*

(7) BUTIR *(a grain)*

This classifier may be used of fruits, coconuts, gems and eggs. Examples:

sebutir pisang	*a banana*
sebutir nyiur	*a coconut*
sebutir permata	*a jewel*
sebutir telur	*an egg*

In all these cases, however, *biji* could be used instead of *butir*.

(8) ÉKOR *(tail)*

This is the classifier for all living creatures except plants and human beings. Examples:

seékor kucing	*a cat*
seékor burung	*a bird*
seékor labah-labah	*a spider*
seékor ikan	*a fish*
seékor ular	*a snake*

(9) HELAI *(colloquially LAI)*

This is a very common classifier for cloth, clothing, grass, hair, leaves, paper. Examples:

sehelai kain	*a length of cloth; a sarong*
sehelai rumput	*a blade of grass*
sehelai rambut	*one strand of hair*
sehelai daun	*a leaf*
sehelai kertas	*a sheet of paper*

(10) KAKI *(foot, leg)*

This is not a very common classifier, but it can be used with flowers, umbrellas. Examples:

sekaki bunga	*a flower*
sekaki payung	*an umbrella*

(11) KAYU *(wood)*

Used with *kain* (cloth) this word means "roll". Example:

sekayu kain	*a roll of cloth*

(12) KEPING *(piece)*

This classifier is quite common and is used of things that come in pieces or lumps. Examples:

sekeping roti	*a piece of bread*
sekeping daging	*a piece of meat*
sekeping kertas	*a piece of paper*

(13) KUNTUM.*(bud)*

This is the normal classifier for flowers. Example:

sekuntum bunga	*a flower*

(14) ORANG *(person)*

This is one of the commonest classifiers and is used of human beings. Examples:

seorang budak	*a youngster*
seorang tukang kebun	*a gardener*

When it would occur in front of itself, *orang* is usually omitted. Examples:

seorang (orang) Cina	*a Chinese*
seorang (orang) perempuan	*a woman*
seorang (orang)	*a person*

(15) PATAH *(broken)*

This classifier is used of words and phrases. Example:

sepatah perkataan	*a word*

(16) PINTU *(door)*

A classifier for houses arranged in rows or terraces—shophouses for instance. Example:

sepintu rumah	*a (terrace) house*

(17) POTONG *(cut off)*

This is used of things cut in slices. Examples:

sepotong daging	*a slice of meat* (cf. *English "a cut off the joint"*)
sepotong roti	*a slice of bread*

(18) PUCUK *(shoot, bud)*

This is quite a common classifier for guns and letters. Examples:

sepucuk senapang	*a gun*
sepucuk surat	*a letter*

(19) PUNTUNG *(stub)*

This classifier is used for the butt-ends of cigars, cigarettes, candles, etc. Examples:

sepuntung rokok	*a cigar-butt;*
	a cigarette-end
sepuntung lilin	*a candle-end*

(20) RAWAN

Used of fishing-nets. Example:

serawan jala	*a casting-net*

(21) TANGGA *(ladder)*

This word is used as a classifier for Malay-style houses which are raised off the ground and entered by means of a ladder of staircase. Example:

setangga rumah Melayu	*a Malay house*

(22) TANGKAI *(stalk, stem)*

This classifier is used of flowers. Example:

setangkai bunga	*a flower*

(23) URAT *(strand)*

Used of thread. Example:

seurat benang	*a strand of thread.*
	a piece of thread

(24) UTAS *(string)*

A classifier for things in strings. Examples:

seutas tali	*a rope*
seutas benang	*a skein of thread*

MALAY NAMES AND TITLES

Most Malay personal names are Arabic in origin and the system of naming a person follows the Judaeo-Arabic system.

Malays do not have surnames or family names. A man has his own name followed by that of his father, the two being joined together by the word *bin* (Arabic: *ibn;* Hebrew: *ben;* Aramaic: *bar);* a woman has the same arrangement except that in her case the two names are joined by the word *binti* (Arabic: *binti), Bin* means "son of" and *binti* means "daughter of". Cf. in the Bible "Simon Bar Joseph" – Simon the son of Joseph.

Suppose a man, *Ibrahim,* has a son called *Yusuf* and a daughter called *Habsah.* The son will be known as *Yusuf bin Ibrahim* and the daughter as *Habsah binti Ibrahim.*

When *Yusuf* gets married and has a son called, say, *Arshad,* the son (i.e. *Ibrahim's* grandson) will be known as *Arshad bin Yusuf.* If *Habsah* marries a man called *Ishak,* and bears a son called *Muhammad,* this grandson of *Ibrahim's* will be known as *Muhammad bin Ishak.* In other words all trace of connexion with *Ibrahim* is erased by the third generation.

When we address Malays in English, we should be careful which name we use after Mr or Mrs. In the above family, *Yusuf* is known as *Mr Yusuf* not as *Mr Ibrahim. Habsah,* when married, will be called *Mrs Ishak* in English.

In Malay all the above names (or any other name for that matter) may carry the prefix *Encik* or *Cik.*

Encik Ibrahim	*Mr Ibrahim*
Encik Yusuf	*Mr Yusuf*
Cik Habsah	*Miss Habsah (before marriage); Mrs Ishak (after marriage)*

Notice that in Malay a woman retains her own name when married. It is only when spoken of in English that she should be addressed as *Mrs Ishak. Cik* is used with the names of women and *Encik* is used with the names of men, although nowadays *Cik* is increasingly used with the names of both men and women.

Now, if *Ibrahim* fulfils his religious duty and makes a successful pilgrimage to Mecca, on his return he will be known as *Haji Ibrahim* (i.e. Pilgrim Ibrahim) and is entitled to be addressed as *Tuan*. His children bask in reflected glory, for they will now be known as *Encik Yusuf bin Haji Ibrahim* and *Cik Habsah binti Haji Ibrahim* respectively.

Another group of people entitled to be addressed as *Tuan* are the Saiyids. A Saiyid (Syed) is of Arab descent and claims to be descended directly from the Prophet Muhammad. He puts the prefix *Saiyid* before his name, e.g. *Saiyid Yusuf bin Saiyid Ibrahim,* and is addressed as *Tuan* or *Tuan Saiyid.*

A *Tengku* (prince or princess) should normally be addressed as *Tengku,* but in conversation *Tuan* would probably be accepted to most.

Malay titles are legion but the above information should be sufficient for everyday purposes.

APPENDIX C

THE MALAY CALENDAR

The Malays use the Muslim calendar which is lunar in origin and is therefore eleven days short of the solar year. As in most Muslim countries, these lunar months are usually known by their Arabic names, although one or two months which are connected with important Islamic festivals have also acquired Malay names which are more commonly used. The months, which have 29 and 30 days alternately, do not correspond in any way with the solar months; indeed, a complicated mathematical process is involved in converting Muslim dates to Christian dates and vice versa. The names of the months are:

(1)	Muharram	30 days
(2)	Safar	29 days
(3)	Rabi-ul-awwal [or: Bulan Maulud: the month in which the Prophet Muhammad was born].	30 days
(4)	Rabi-ul-akhir	29 days
(5)	Jamad-il-awal	30 days
(6)	Jamad-il-akhir	29 days
(7)	Rejab	30 days
(8)	Syaaban	29 days
(9)	Ramdan [or: Bulan Puasa: the fasting month]	30 days
(10)	Syawal [or: Bulan Raya: the month of feasting which follows the fast]	29 days
(11)	Dzul-kaedah	30 days
(12)	Dzul-hijjah	29 days

MALAY SOLECISMS

This appendix deals with some of the common fallacies of Bazaar Malay. These forms are used by many people who are labouring under the delusion that they are speaking "colloquial" Malay. Malays only use these forms when talking down to foreigners under the mistaken impression that they are easier to understand.

If a Malay uses these forms in conversation with you, try to persuade him that you know better. If a non-Malay tells you that any of these forms are correct, you should at once become suspicious of anything else he tells you about the language because his knowledge of Malay will definitely be below standard. No Malay would ever use these ugly forms in conversation with another Malay, except jocularly. This kind of Malay is no better than pidgin.

(1) BANYAK

This word does not mean "very" "Very good" is not *banyak baik*, but *sangat baik* or *baik sungguh*. *Banyak* is a noun, not an adverb. To say *banyak baik* is as bad as saying "plenty good" in English.

(2) PUNYA

This word, which is rarely heard at all in real Malay, is often used in Bazaar Malay in imitation of a Chinese construction to indicate possession. Examples:

saya punya rumah	*my house*
dia punya bapa punya keréta	*his father's car*

These forms are quite incorrect. You should say:

rumah saya	*my house*
keréta bapa dia	*his father's car*

(3) SAMA

Sama is often used in Bazaar Malay to indicate a direct or indirect object:

saya téngok sama dia	*I saw him*
saya bagi duit sama dia	*I gave him the money*

This usage is wrong. There is no need for the word at all in the first example: in the second it should be either left out (with a change in word order) or changed to *kepada:*

saya téngok dia	*I saw him*
saya bagi dia duit	
or: saya bagi duit kepada dia	*I gave him the money*

(4) KASI

Kasi does not mean "to give"; it means "to castrate". It is difficult to understand how such an unpleasant word has come to be used so frequently with an entirely wrong meaning. In written Malay the correct word for "to give" is *beri* or *berikan*. These, however, sound a bit bookish and are usually replaced in real colloquial Malay by *bagi*.

(5) BILANG

Bilang does not mean "to say"; it means "to count". Therefore such a sentence as

saya sudah bilang sama dia   *I said to him*

should be

saya sudah kata kepada dia   *I said to him*

(6) PERGI

This word is not pronounced "piggy" or "pigi" or "piki". The *-r-* is silent in all but very formal speech. The normal pronunciation is *pegi* (with the stress on *-gi*). In very rapid speech it becomes *pi* or *gi*.

(7) BIKIN

Bikin has no meaning at all. It cannot be used as a synonym for *buat*.

(8) TADA

This is another word which does not exist in real Malay. In Bazaar Malay, however, it is used in place of both *tidak* and *tak ada*. This usage is wrong. The glottal catch in *tak ada* is never omitted by a Malay speaker, and the short form of *tidak* is either *tak* or *dak* according to the context.

(9) MAHU

Mahu should never be used to form a future tense; the correct form for this is *hendak* (colloquially: *nak*). Cf. Grammar sections (62) and (63) in Lesson 23.

(10) KECIL

This word is not pronounced "kitchy". In careful speech it is pronounced exactly as spelt and in colloquial language it usually becomes *kecik* or *keci'*.

(11) SETENGAH

This is often used in Malayan English to mean "a whisky and soda", i.e. half a tot. In English pronunciation this has become "stinger", which is all right in English. Don't, however, import this pronunciation back into Malay. In rapid speech the -*e*- of *se*- usually drops out and so this word is usually pronounced *stengah*, but never *stinger*.

CLASSIFIED VOCABULARIES

This Appendix contains a number of short vocabularies of essential words arranged according to topics. You are recommended to work through these lists of words making up at least two sentences for each word to help you to remember them.

Colours **Warna**

black, hitam
blue, biru
brown, perang
green, hijau
grey, kelabu
red, mérah
saffron, kunyit

yellow, kuning
white, putih
light (of colours), muda
dark (of colours), tua
   e.g. *light blue*, biru muda
       dark red, mérah tua

Parts of the Body **Bahagian Badan**

arm, lengan
chest, dada
ear, telinga
eye, mata
face, muka
finger, jari
foot, kaki
hair, rambut
hand, tangan
head, kepala

leg, kaki
mouth, mulut
nail, kuku
neck, léhér
nose, hidung
thumb, ibu jari
toe, ibu jari kaki
tooth, gigi
waist, pinggang

Clothing **Pakaian**

belt, talipinggang

jacket, baju

brassière, baju dalam (péndék)
coat, baju
dress (woman's), gaun
gloves, sarungtangan
handkerchief, saputangan
hat (general term), topi
hat (Malay style), songkok
sleeve, tangan
slip (woman's), baju dalam
    (panjang)
socks, sarungkaki (péndék)
stockings, sarungkaki (panjang)
tie, taliléhér

nightdress, baju tidur
panties (women's) seluar dalam
pyjamas, baju tidur
sarong, kain; kain sarung
shirt, baju keméja
shoes, kasut
shorts, seluar péndék
trousers, seluar panjang
turban, serban
underpants, seluar dalam
undervest, baju dalam
long, panjang
short, péndék

Animals, Birds, Insects, etc.   Binatang, Burung, Serangga, d.s.b.*

Animals, Binatang
 buffalo, kerbau
 cat, kucing
 civet-cat, musang
 cow, lembu (betina)
 dog, anjing
 elephant, gajah
 gibbon, wak-wak
 goat, kambing
 horse, kuda
 house-lizard (gecko), cicak
 lion, singa
 monkey, kera
 mouse, tikus
 mouse-deer, pelanduk
 ox, lembu (jantan)
 pig, babi
 rat, tikus
 snake, ular
 tiger, harimau; rimau
Birds, Burung
 chicken, ayam

crow, burung gagak
duck, itik
goose, angsa
turkey, ayam Belanda
Insects, etc., Serangga, d.s.b.
 ant, semut
 bee, lebah
 beetle, kumbang
 centipede, lipan
 cicada, riang-riang
 cockroach, lipas
 fire-fly, kelip-kelip
 fly, lalat
 hornet, tebuan
 mantis, cencada
 mason-bee, angkut-angkut
 mosquito, nyamuk
 scorpion, kala
 spider, labah-labah
 wasp, penyengat
 white ants, anai-anai

* d.s.b. is short for *dan sebagainya* (and things like that) which is
equivalent to etcetera.

Malayan Geography 'Ilmu Bumi Malaya

Federation of Malaya, Persekutuan Tanah Melayu
Johore, negeri Johor
Kedah, negeri Kedah
Kelantan, negeri Kelantan
Malacca, negeri Melaka
Negri Sembilan, Negeri Sembilan
Pahang, negeri Pahang
Penang (State), negeri Pinang
Penang (Island), Pulau Pinang
Perak, negeri Pérak
Perlis, negeri Perlis
Province Wellesley, * Seberang Perai
Selangor, negeri Selangor
Trengganu, negeri Trengganu
bay, teluk
confluence, kuala
estuary, kuala
fort, kota
headland, tanjung
island, pulau

mountain, gunung
peninsula, semenanjung
point, tanjung
river, sungai
rubber, getah
rubber estate, kebun getah
rubber-tapper, penoréh getah
rubber-tree, pokok getah
(to) tap rubber, toréh getah
tree, pokok
rice (growing), padi
rice (uncooked), beras
rice (cooked), nasi
rice-field, bendang; sawah
tin, biji timah
cloud, awan
dew, embun
floods, air bah
lightning, kilat
mist, kabut
rain, hujan
storm, ribut
thunder, guruh-gemuruh

* Now included in the State of Penang.

House and Garden Rumah dan Kebun

House, Rumah
chick (window blind), bidai
door, pintu
drain, parit, longkang
fence, pagar
garden, kebun
gardener, tukang kebun
roof, bumbung
storey, tingkat
verandah (European style), beranda

bed-room, bilik tidur
bed (general term), tempat tidur
bed (European style), katil
bed (sleeping platform as used in servants' quarters), pangking
blanket, selimut bulu
mattress, tilam
mosquito-net, kelambu
pillow, bantal
sheet, selimut

verandah (Malay style), serambi
wall (outside wall), témbok
wall (partition wall) dinding
window, tingkap

dining-room, bilik makan
chair, kerusi
fork, garfu
knife, pisau
spoon, camca
table, méja
cook (n.), kuki
crockery; pinggan mangkuk
cup, cawan
frying-pan, kuali
kettle, cérek
maidservant, amah

wardrobe, almari

bathroom, bilik air; bilik mandi
bucket, timba
dipper, timba
soap, sabun
tap, pili
toilet (W.C.), jamban
towel, tuala
water, air
kitchen, dapur
bowl, mangkuk
plate, pinggan
saucer, piring
stove, dapur
wash the clothes, cuci kain
wash up the dishes, cuci
pinggan

Food and Cooking   Makanan Dan Masak

NOUNS:
bean, kacang
beef, daging lembu
bread, roti
butter, mentéga
cabbage, kobis
cheese, kéju
chicken, ayam
chillies, cabai
coffee, kopi
crab, ketam
curry, gulai
duck, itik
egg, telur
fish, ikan
flour, tepung
French beans, kacang buncis
lady's fingers, kacang bendi
meat, daging
milk, susu

mutton, daging kambing
onion, bawang
peas, kacang pea
pepper, lada putih
potato, ubi; ubi kentang
pork, daging babi
prawn, udang
rice (growing), padi
rice (uncooked), beras
rice (cooked), nasi
sago, sagu
salt, garam
soya beans, kacang soya
soya sauce, tauyu; kicap
sugar, gula
tapioca, ubi kayu
tea (liquid), téh
tea (in leaf form), daun téh
vinegar, cuka

ADJECTIVES:
  bitter, pahit
  cold, sejuk
  hot (temperature), hangat
  hot (peppery), pedas
  raw, mentah
  ready, siap
  ripe, masak
  sour, masam
  sweet, manis
  tasteless, tawar
  tasty, sedap

VERBS:
  boil, rebus
  cook, masak
  fry, goréng
  roast, panggang

APPENDIX F

MALAY-ENGLISH VOCABULARY

The following vocabulary contains all the words in the course arranged alphabetically. The Arabic numerals in round brackets, e.g. (123), refer to the grammar sections in the body of the course. If you find a number like this next to a word in the vocabulary, it means that it is definitely unsafe to use that word without first consulting the appropriate grammar section.

ada, *to be, to exist; to have;* (22)
agung, *general*
Ahad, cf. hari Ahad
air, *water*
air bah, *floods*
akhir, *end*
alih, *to move* (transitive)
almari, *cupboard, wardrobe*
Alor Setar, *Alor Star* (36a)
ambil, *to take; to fetch, to get*
amah, *maidservant*
anak, *child, offspring, son, daughter*
anak perempuan, *daughter*
angkut-angkut, *mason-bee*

angsa, *goose*
anjing, *dog*
antara, *between, among* (133)
apa, *what* (12)
apa-apa, *anything* (128)
apa khabar? *how are you?* (19)
api, *fire*
asing, *separate* (adj.); *foreign*
atas, *top* (132)
awan, *cloud*
ayam, *chicken*
ayam Belanda, *turkey* (lit. Dutch chicken)
anak laki-laki, *son*

B

babi, *pig*
baca, *to read*
badan, *body*
bagi, *to give; for; to let, allow; to make, cause* (143)
bagi pinjam, *to lend* (142) (143)

bagus, *splendid, fine, beautiful, excellent*
bahagian, *part*
baharu, *new; newly; only just, only then*
bahasa, *language*

bahasa Cina, *Chinese*
bahasa Inggeris, *English* (31)
bahasa kebangsaan, *national language*
bahasa Melayu, *Malay*
bahasa orang putih, *English* (31)
bahasa Tamil, *Tamil*
baik, *good; had better* (39)
baiklah, *all right, O.K.* (37)
baju, *coat, jacket, blouse*
baju dalam, *undervest*
baju dalam panjang, (woman's) *slip*
baju dalam péndék, *brassière*
baju keméja, *shirt*
baju tidur, *nightdress; pyjamas*
balik, *to return, to go back, to come back; to go home, to come home*
bancuh, *to mix; to make* (coffee, cocoa); *to pour out* (tea); (113)
bancuh kopi, *to make coffee*
bancuh téh, *to pour out the tea*
bangun, *to get up, to rise*
bangunan, *building*
bantal, *pillow; loaf*
banyak, *a lot of; much, many* (25); cf. Appendix D (1)
bapa, *father*
barang, *thing, goods, luggage*
barangkali, *perhaps*
bas, *bus* (134)
basah, *wet*
basikal, *bicycle*
bawa, *to bring, to carry, to lead; to take a person*
bawa keréta, *to drive a car*
bawah, *underneath* (132)
bawang, *onion*
bayar, *to pay*
béca, *rickshaw, trishaw*
bekerja, *to work*
bekerja kuat, *to work hard*

belah, cf. **sebelah**
belajar, *to learn, to study*
belakang, *back, behind* (132)
belanja, *expense, cost*
beli, *to buy*
belum, *not, not yet* (110–111)
benang, *thread*
bendang, *rice-field, padi-field*
bentuk, *curve; cl. for rings and hooks*
beranda, *verandah* (European style)
berapa, *how much, how many* (50)
berapa lama, *how long* (in time)
beras, *rice* (uncooked but not growing)
berbahaya, *dangerous*
berbual-bual, *to have a chat*
bercakap, *to talk, to speak*
bercukur, *to shave* (oneself); *to have a shave*
bercuti, *to be on leave, to go on leave*
berdiri, *to stand, to stand up*
berenang, *to swim*
berguna, *useful*
berhenti, *to stop*
berhutang, *indebted; to be in debt, to owe*
berjalan, *to walk, to go, to be under way* (141)
berjalan-jalan, *to walk about*
berjalan kaki, *to walk, to go on foot*
berkahwin, *married; to be married, to get married*
berkata, *to say*
berlari, *to run*
bermain, *to play*
bermalam, *to spend the night*
berpindah, *to move* (house)

bersanding, *to sit side by side in state; bersanding* (109)

bersembunyi, *to hide* (intransitive)

bersetuju, *to agree*

bertanya, *to ask, to inquire*

bertolak, *to start, to leave; to set sail; to move off*

berumur, *to be aged ...; to be ... (years, etc.) old*

besar, *big, large, great*

besar hati, *proud* (in a good sense) (106)

bésok, *tomorrow*

bétina, *female, feminine* (13)

biasanya, *usually*

bidai, *chick, window-blind*

bidang, *broad; cl. for sails, mats, etc.*

biji, *seed; cl. for small objects,* (48)

bijih timah, *tin, tin ore*

bikin, cf. Appendix D (7)

bila, *when*

bilah, *narrow strip; cl. for knives etc.*

bilang, *to count;* cf. Appendix D (5)

bilik, *room, bedroom*

bilik air, *bathroom*

bilik makan, *dining-room*

bilik mandi, *bathroom*

bilik tidur, *bedroom*

binatang, *animal*

biru, *blue*

bodoh, *stupid*

bola, *ball*

bola golf, *golf-ball*

bolasépak, *football*

boléh, *can, to be able*

buah, *fruit; cl. for large objects* (47)

buah-buahan, *all kinds of fruit*

buah durian, *durian*

buah limau, *orange*

buah manggis, *mangosteen*

buah pinang, *areca nut, betel nut*

buah pisang, *banana*

buah rambutan, *rambutan*

buat, *to make, to do*

bubuh, *to put, to place*

budak, *youngster; boy; girl*

budak laki-laki, *boy*

budak perempuan, *girl*

buka, *to open*

bukan, *no, not* (2)

bukit, *hill*

buku, *book*

bulan, *month; moon*

bulan-bulan, *every month*

bulan depan, *next month*

bulan lepas, *last month*

bumbung, *roof*

bunga, *flower*

burung, *bird*

burung gagak, *crow* (n.)

butir, (a.) *grain; cl. for fruits, gems, etc.*

C

cabai, *chillies*

camca, *spoon*

cantik, *pretty, beautiful*

cari, *to seek, to look for*

cawan, *cup*

cencada, *mantis*

cepat, *fast, quick, quickly*

cérék, *kettle*

cicak, *house-lizard, gecko*

Cina, *Chinese*

cincin, *ring*
cuba, *to try*
cuci, *to clean*
cuci kain, *to wash the clothes,
    to do the washing*

cuci pinggan, *to wash the
    dishes; to do the washing-up*
cuka, *vinegar*
cukai, *duty, tax; customs*
cukur, *to shave* (transitive)
cukup, *enough, sufficient*

D

dada, *chest*
daging, *meat, flesh*
daging babi, *pork*
daging kambing, *mutton*
daging lembu, *beef*
dahulu, *previously, before,
    earlier, ago, first*
dalam, *in, inside*
dan, *and;*
dan lagi, *also, in addition,
    furthermore*
dan sebagainya, *and so on,
    etcetera*
dapat, *to get, to obtain; to
    manage to; to receive*
dapur, *kitchen*
dari, *from* (35a) (92)
dari mana, *where ... from;
    from where; whence*
daripada, *from* (35a) (92)
dari sana, *from there; thence*
datang, *to come* (41)
datang sama, *to come too*
daun, *leaf*
daun téh, *tea* (dry leaves)
dakwat, *ink*
delapan, *eight*
delapan belas, *eighteen*
delapan puluh, *eighty*

demam, *fever; to have a
    fever*
denda, *fine* (n.)
dengan, *with*
dengar, *to hear; to listen to*
depan, *next; front* (132)
di, *in, at* (14)
dia, *he, she; him, her; his, her*
    (17)
dia sendiri, *he himself; she
    herself*
dilahirkan, *to be born*
di luar, *outside*
di mana, *where*
dinding, (partition) *wall*
di rumah, *at home*
di sana, *there; over there*
di sini, *here*
doktor, *doctor*
d.s.b. (dan sebagainya), *etc.*
dua, *two*
dua belas, *twelve*
dua puluh, *twenty*
duduk, *to sit, to stay, to live,
    to dwell* (33)
duit, *money*
dulu, *previously, before, earlier,
    ago, first*
durian, cf. buah durian

E

ékor, *tail;* cl. *for animals* (46)
elektrik, *electric*
emak, *mother*
embun, *dew*
empat, *four*
empat belas, *fourteen*
empat puluh, *forty*

enam, *six*
enam belas, *sixteen*
enam puluh, *sixty*
encik, *you, your* (17) (27)
ésok, *tomorrow*

G

gajah, *elephant*
gaji, *salary, wages, pay*
gambar, *picture*
gantung, *to hang*
garam, *salt*
garfu, *fork*
gaun, (woman's) *dress*
gelas, *glass*
gelap, *dark*
gemuk, *fat*
gereja, *church*

getah, *rubber*
gi, *to go*
gigi, *tooth*
goréng, *to fry*
gula, *sugar*
gulai, *curry*
gunung, *mountain*
guru, *teacher*
guru besar, *headmaster,*
    headmistress
guruh-gemuruh, *thunder*

H

habis, *finish, finished*
harga, *price*
harganya, *cost* (56)
hari, *day*
hari Ahad, *Sunday*
hari Senin, *Monday*
hari ini, *today*
hari Jumaat, *Friday*
hari Khamis, *Thursday*
harimau, *tiger*
hari Rabu, *Wednesday*
hari Sabtu, *Saturday*
hari Selasa, *Tuesday*

hangat, *hot* (general term)
    (70)
hati, *liver; "heart"*
    (106)
helai, cl. *for cloth, clothes;* cf.
    Appendix A
hendak, *to be going to, to intend*
    to, will, shall (62)
hidung, *nose*

hidup, *to live,* (to be) *alive* (33)
hijau, *green*
Hindu, *Hindu* (adj.)
hisap, *to smoke*
hitam, *black*
hujan, *rain*

hukum, *sentence* (legal)
hukum gantung, *sentence of death (by hanging)*
hutan, *jungle, forest*
hutang, *debt*

I

ibu jari, *thumb*
ikan, *fish*
ilmu bumi, *geography*
ikut, *to follow; according to*
ikut ini, *this way* (direction)
ikut itu, *that way* (direction)
India, *India, Indian* (adj.)

ingat, *to think; to remember*
Inggeris, *English* (adj.)
ini, *this, these*
isteri, *wife*
istiadat, *ceremony*
itik, *duck*
itu, *that, those*

J

jadi, *to become*
jahat *wicked*
jala, *casting-net*
jalan, *road, way*
jam, *hour; watch, clock*
jamban, *toilet, W.C.*
jangan, *don't* (146)
jangan sekali-kali, cf. (149)
jangan tidak, cf. (148)
jantan, *male, masculine* (13)
jantung, *heart (106)*
jari, *finger*

jari kaki, *toe*
jarum, *needle*
jemput, *to ask, to invite*
Jepun, *Japan, Japanese* (adj.)
Johor, *Johore*
Johor Baharu, *Johore Bahru*
jual, *to sell*
juga, *all the same* (121) (136) (137) (139)
Jumaat, cf. hari Jumaat
juta, *million*

K

kabut, *mist*
kacang, *bean*
kacang bendi, *lady's fingers*
kacang buncis, *French beans*

kacang hijau, *peas*
kacang soya, *soya beans*
kah, *question particle* (118)
kail, *fish-hook*

kain, *cloth; sarong*
kain sarung, *sarong*
kajang, *palm frond; cadjan, attap*
kaki, *foot, leg;* cl. *for flowers*
kala, *scorpion*
kalam, *pen*
kalau, *if*
kali, *time, occasion*
kambing, *goat*
kampung, *village; compound*
kapal, *ship*
kapal api, *steamship*
kapalterbang, *aeroplane*
karangan, *essay, composition*
kasih, *love* (n.)
kasihan, *pity*
kasihan dia!, *poor fellow!*
kasi, cf. Appendix D (4)
kasut, *shoe*
kata, *to say*
kata kepada, *to tell, inform*
kati, *catty* (one and one-third pounds avoirdupoids)
katil, *bed* (European style)
kawan, *friend*
kaya, *rich*
kayu, *wood; roll* (of cloth)
ke, *to* (34a)
kebangsaan, *national*
kebun, *garden, estate*
kebun getah, *rubber estate*
kecil, *little, small*
kecil hati, *hurt* (of feelings)
Kedah, *Kedah*
kedai, *shop*
kedai buku, *bookshop*
kedai daging, *butcher's shop*
kedai kopi, *coffee-shop; café*
kedai makan, *restaurant*
keju, *cheese*
kelabu, *grey*
kelambu, *mosquito-net*

Kelantan, *Kelantan*
kelip-kelip, *firefly*
kelmarin dahulu, *the day before yesterday*
keluar, *to go out, to come out*
ke mana, *where ...to; whither*
kemerdékaan, *independence*
kena, *to incur, to be affected by* (120)
kena cukai, (to be) *dutiable,* (to be) *taxable*
kena denda, *to be fined*
kena hukum, *to be sentenced* (to)
kena hukum gantung, *to be sentenced to death*
kena langgar keréta, *to get run over*
kena luka, *to be wounded, to be injured*
kena tangkap, *to be arrested, to get caught*
kenduri, *feast; party*
kepada, *to* (34a)
kepala, *head*
keping, *piece, lump*
kera, *monkey*
kerajaan, *government*
kerana, *because*
kerbau, *buffalo*
keréta, *vehicle; car; cart*
kerétapi, *railway train*
keréta lembu, *bullock cart*
keréta séwa, *taxi; hire-car*
kering, *dry*
kerja, *work* (n.)
kertas, *paper*
kertas tulis, *writing-paper*
kerusi, *chair*
ke sana, (to) *there, thither*
ke sini, (to) *here, hither*
ketam, *crab*
khabar, *news*

khabar baik, *I'm fine* (19)
Khamis, cf. hari Khamis
kilat, *lightning*
kita, *we, us; our* (17)
kobis, *cabbage*
kopi, *coffee*
kosong, *'empty; nought, nil, zero*
kota, *fort*
Kota Baharu, *Kota Bharu*
kotak, (small) *box*
kotor, *dirty*
kuala, *estuary, confluence*
kuali, *frying-pan*

kuat, *strong*
kucing, *cat*
kuda, *horse*
kuil, (Hindu) *temple*
kuki, *cook* (n.)
kuku, (finger-, toe-) *nail*
kumbang, *beetle*
kuning, *yellow*
kuntum, *bud;* cl. *for flowers*
kunyit, *saffron*
kupang, *ten cents* (North Malaya)
kurang, *less, minus* (103)
kurus, *thin*

L

labah-labah, *spider*
lada putih, *pepper*
lagi, *else, more, still, yet*
lagi ... lagi ..., *the more ... the more ...*
lagi suka, *to prefer*
lah, *emphatic particle* (37)
lai, cl. *for cloth, clothing, etc.,* cf. Appendix A
lain, *different*
lain kali, *next time, another time*
laki-laki, *male, masculine* (13)
lalat, *fly* (n.)
lama, *long* (of time); *old* (of things) (123)
lambat, *late; slow* (100)
lambat-lambat, *slowly*
langgar, *collision*
lantai, *floor*
lapan, *eight*
lapan belas, *eighteen*
lapan puluh, *eighty*
lari, *to run away*

laut, *sea*
lebah, *bee*
lebih, *more, in excess*
lebih kurang, *approximately, more or less*
léhér, *neck*
lekas, *immediately, at once; quickly*
lemari, *cupboard, wardrobe*
lembu, *ox, cow*
léngah, *to idle, to hang about*
lengan, *arm*
lepas, *after, beyond; last* (preceding)
lepas itu, *after that, afterwards*
léwat, *late, too late* (100)
lilin, *candle*
lima, *five*
lima belas, *fifteen*
lima puluh, *fifty*
limau, cf. buah limau
lipan, *centipede*
lipas, *cockroach*

lobang, *hole*
lombong, *mine*
lombong bijih timah, *tin-mine*
lompat, *to jump*

loteri, *lottery*
lulus dalam, *to pass*
(examinations)
lusa, *the day after tomorrow*

M

maafkan, *to excuse, to forgive*
macam, *kind, sort; like, as, as if*
macam ini, *like this, this way*
macam itu, *like that, that way*
macam mana, *how*
mahal, *dear, expensive*
Maha Mulia, cf. Yang Maha Mulia
mahu, *to want;* cf. Appendix D (9)
makan, *to eat*
makanan, *food*
makan pagi, *breakfast; to have breakfast*
malam, *night, evening* (97) (124)
malas, *lazy*
Malaya, *Malaya*
mana, *which*
mana-mana, *any* (adj.) (128)
mandi, *to have a bath; to bathe; to wash*
manggis, cf. buah manggis
mangkuk, *bowl*
manis, *sweet*
marah, *angry*
mari, *to come* (41)
masa, *time; while, when* (105)
masak, *ripe; to cook*
masam, *sour*

masuk, *to go in, to come in, to enter*
mata, *eye*
matahari, *sun*
mata-mata, *policeman*
mati, *to die; to be dead; dead*
méja, *table*
Melaka, *Malacca*
Melayu, *Malay* (adj.)
menang, *to win*
menengah, *secondary* (education)
menjawab, *to answer, to reply*
mentah, *raw*
mentéga, *butter*
mérah, *red*
merdéka, *independent* (91)
mesjid, *mosque*
minggu, *week*
minggu depan, *next week*
minggu lepas, *last week*
minit, *minute* (n.)
minta, *to ask for, to demand*
minum, *to drink*
miskin, *poor*
muda, *young*
mujur, *lucky, fortunate*
mujurlah!, *that's lucky!*
muka, *face*
mula, *to begin* (96)
mulai, *to begin* (96)
mula-mula, *at first; originally*
mulut, *mouth*
murah, *cheap*
musang, *civet-cat*
muzium, *museum*

N

naik, *to go up, to ascend; to mount; to ride* (in, on) (40)

nak, *to be going to, to intend to; will, shall* (62)

nak ke, *to be off to* (64)

nama, *name*

nampak, *to see, to catch sight of* (42)

nanti, *to wait* (108)

nantikan, *to wait for* (108)

nasi, *rice* (cooked)

negeri, *state, country*

Negeri China, *China*

Negeri Johor, *Johore*

Negeri Kedah, *Kedah*

Negeri Kelantan, *Kelantan*

Negeri Melaka, *Malacca*

Negeri Pahang, *Pahang*

Negeri Perak, *Perak*

Negeri Perlis, *Perlis*

Negeri Pinang, *Penang*

Negeri Selangor, *Selangor*

Negeri Sembilan, *Negri Sembilan* (125)

Negeri Trengganu, *Trengganu*

nombor, *number*

nombor satu, *first-class, best quality*

nya, *his, her, its* (56)

nyamuk, *mosquito*

nyiur, *coconut*

O

orang, *man, woman, person;* cl. *for human beings* (45)

orang Cina, *a Chinese*

orang gaji, *servant, employee*

orang Hindu, *a Hindu*

orang Jepun, *a Japanese*

orang kedai, *shopkeeper*

orang laki-laki, *man*

orang Melayu, *a Malay*

orang perempuan, *woman*

orang Portugis, *a Portuguese*

orang putih, *a European*

orang sakit, *sick person; patient* (n.)

P

pada, *on, at* (time)

padi, *rice* (growing)

pagar, *fence*

pagi, *morning* (refers only to the past)

pahit, *bitter*

pakai, *to use; to wear, to put on*

pakaian, *clothes, clothing*

panas, *hot* (sun) (70)

pandai, *clever, good at*

panggang, *to roast*

pangking, *bed; wooden sleeping platform as used in servants' quarters,etc.*

panjang, *long*

pantai, *beach, shore*

parit, *ditch, drain*

pasal, *concerning, about*

pasal apa, *why*

pasar, *market, bazaar*

pasar buah-buahan, *fruit-market*

pasir, *sand*

patah, *broken, fractured;* cl. *for words and phrases*

payah, cf. *tak payah*

payung, *umbrella*

pedang, *sword*

pedas, *hot* (of curry)

pejabat, *office*

pejabat pos, *post office*

pekan, *town*

pekerja, *worker, employee*

pelajaran, *lesson; education*

pelajaran ulangkaji, *revision lesson*

pelamin, *bridal throne* (109)

pelanduk, *mousedeer*

pencen, *pension*

péndék, *short*

pengantin, *bride; bridegroom*

pengantin laki-laki, *bridegroom*

pengantin perempuan, *bride*

pengganas, *terrorist; bandit*

penjahat, *terrorist; bandit*

penjara, *prison, gaol*

penumpang, *passenger*

penoréh getah, *rubber-tapper*

penyakit, *disease, illness*

penyengat, *wasp*

peperiksaan, *examination*

pérang, *brown*

perempuan, *female, feminine* (13)

pergi, *to go;* cf. Appendix D (6)

pergi lekas, *to go at once; to hurry*

pergi sama, *to go too*

perkataan, *word*

Perlis, *Perlis*

permata, *jewel*

persekutuan, *federation; federal*

pertama, *first* (93a)

perut, *stomach*

petang, *afternoon, evening* (124)

pi, *to go* (especially in Kedah and the North generally)

pili, *tap* (n.)

pinang, cf. buah pinang

Pinang, *Penang*

pinggan, *plate, dish*

pinggan mangkuk, *crockery*

pinjam, *to borrow* (142)

pinjamkan, *to lend* (142)

pintu, *door;* cl. *for terrace houses*

piring, *saucer*

pisang, cf. buah pisang

pisau, *knife*

pisau cukur, *razor*

pokét, *pocket*

pokok, *tree*

pokok getah, *rubber-tree*

Portugis, *Portuguese* (adj.)

Pos, *Post*

potong, *to cut off; slice,* cf. Appendix A (17)

pucuk, *shoot, bud;* cl. *for letters, needles and guns*

pula, cf. (137) (138)

pulau, *island*

Pulau Pinang, *Penang* (Island) (82)

pukul, *to strike, to beat;*
   o'clock (94)

pun, cf. (129) (130)

...pun...juga, *also, too* (150)

puntung, *stub, butt-end,* cf.
   Appendix A

punya, cf. Appendix' D (2)

putih, *white*

R

Rabu, cf, hari Rabu

raja, *prince; rajah*

rajin, *diligent; hardworking*

ramai, *many* (25)

rambut, *hair*

rambutan, cf. buah
   rambutan

ratus, *hundred*

rawan, cl. *for fishing-nets,* cf.
   Appendix A

rebus, *to boil*

rendah, *low; primary* (education)

riang-riang, *cicada*

ribu, *thousand*

ribut, *storm*

rimau, *tiger*

rimba, *jungle, forest*

ringgit, *dollar*

rokok, *cigar, cigarette*

roti, *bread; loaf*

rumah, *house, building*

rumah sakit, *hospital*

rumput, *grass*

S

saat, *second* (time)

Sabtu, cf. hari Sabtu

sabun, *soap*

sagu, *sago*

sahaja, *only*

sakit, *ill, sick*

sakit hati, *angry*

sakit teruk, *seriously ill*

salah, *wrong, guilty*

sama *together* (with), *along*
   (with); *same; too;* cf. *Appendix*
   D (3)

sama-sama, *same to you; not at
   all; don't mention it* (79)

sampai, *to reach, to arrive; until*

sangat, *very, very much; too* (59)

saputangan, *handkerchief*

sarung, *sheath*

sarungkaki panjang, *stockings*

sarungkaki péndék, *socks*

satu, *one* (44)

sawah, *rice-field, padi-field*

saya, *I, me; my* (17)

saya sendiri, *I myself*

se, *one; a. an* (44)

sebab *cause, motive; because*

sebelah, *beside, next door to, next
   to* (133)

sebelas, *eleven*

sebelum, *before* (time)

Seberang Perai, *Province
   Wellesley*

sedap, *tasty; good* (of food)

segan, *bashful, shy*

sejuk, *cold*
sejuta, *one million*
sekali, *once*
sekali-kali, *at all* (149)
sekali lagi, *once more; again*
sekarang, *now*
sekejap, *a moment*
sekejap lagi, *in a little while, soon*
sekolah, *school*
sekolah, *secondary school*
sekolah rendah *primary school*
sekolah tinggi, *university*
selalu, *always, usually; often*
selamat, *peace; safety* (26); *safe*
selamat jalan, *good-bye* (26)
selamat tinggal, *good-bye* (26)
Selangor, *Selangor*
Selasa, cf. hari Selasa
selimpat, *braided ribbon pattern in lace;* cf. ular selimpat
selimut, *sheet*
selimut, bulu, *blanket*
seluar dalam, *panties* (women's); *underpants* (men's)
seluar panjang, *trousers*
seluar péndék, *shorts*
semacam, *the same; like*
semalam, *yesterday*
sembahyang, *to pray; prayer*
sembilan, *nine*
sembilan belas, *nineteen*
sembilan puluh, *ninety*
semenanjung, *peninsula*
semua, *all* (144)
semut, *ant*
sen, *cent*
senang, *easy*
senapang, *gun*
sendiri, *self*
Senin, cf. hari Senin
seorang, *alone, by oneself*
sépak, *to kick*
sepuluh, *ten*

serambi, *verandah* (Malay style)
serangga, *insect*
seratus *one hundred*
serban, *turban*
seribu, *one thousand*
setengah, *a half;* cf. Appendix D (11)
séwa, *to hire*
siap, *ready*
siapa, *who, whom*
siapa-siapa, *anyone, anybody* (128)
siaran, *broadcast* (n.); (radio) *programme*
sihat, *fit, well, healthy*
sikit, *a little, a bit; rather* (83)
simpan, *to put away, to keep, to store*
simpan duit, *to save money*
singa, *lion*
Singapura, *Singapore*
singgah, *to call in, to stop off*
songkok, *hat* (Malay style)
sudah, *finished, completed* (110) (111)
sudah habis, *all gone, over* (adv.)
suka, *to like*
suka hati, *pleased, happy*
suka tak suka, *willy-nilly* (121)
suku, *quarter*
sultan, *sultan*
sungai, *river*
sungguh, *real, really, very; true*
surat, *letter*
suratkhabar, *newspaper*
suruh, *to tell, to order, to command*
susah, *difficult*
susah hati, *worried, anxious*
susu, *milk*

T

tada, cf. appendix D (8)
tadi, *just now*
tahan, *to hold out, to stand,
to endure; to last*
tahan belanja, *to be able
to afford*
tahu, *to know* (a fact);
to know how to
tahun, *year*
tahun depan, *next year*
tahun lepas, *last year*
tak, *no, not* (7)
tak apa, *it doesn't matter*
(French: ca ne fait rien) (71)
tak berapa, *not very*
tak payah, *there's no need
to; don't bother to* (147c)
tak sempat, *no time (to do)*
takut, *to fear, to be afraid;
frightened*
tali, *string, rope, cord*
taliléhér, *necktie*
talipinggang, *belt*
tanah, *land, earth*
Tanah Melayu, *Malaya*
tangan, *hand, arm; sleeve*
tangga, *ladder; stairs,
staircase* cl. *for Malay style
houses on stilts*
tanjung, *headland, point*
Tanjung, *Georgetown;
Penang* (82)
tangkai, *stalk, stem;* cl.
for flowers
tangkap, *to catch, to arrest*
tapi, *but*
tauyu, *soya-bean sauce*
tawar, *tasteless*
tebuan, *hornet*

téh, *tea* (to drink)
telinga, *ear*
teluk, *bay*
telur, *egg*
témbak, *to shoot, to fire*
témbok, (outside) *wall*
tempat, *place*
tempat tidur, *bed* (general
term)
tengah, *middle* (133)
téngok, *to look at, to see,
to watch* (42)
tentu, *certain, certainly*
tepi, *edge, side* (133)
tepung, *flour*
terbakar, *to be burned down;
to catch fire*
terbang, *to fly*
terbit, *to rise* (of the sun);
to be issued (of books)
terbuka, *open* (adj.)
terima, *to receive*
terima kasih, *thank you* (36)
terjatuh, *to fall down*
terjatuh tangga, *to fall
downstairs*
terlupa, *to forget*
teruk, *acute, severe, arduous*
tetapi, *but*
tiap-tiap, *every, each*
tiba, *to arrive*
tiba-tiba, *suddenly*
tidak, *no, not* (7)
tidur, *to sleep; to go to sleep;
to go to bed*
tiga, *three*
tiga belas, *thirteen*
tiga puluh, *thirty*
tikus, *rat, mouse*
tilam, *mattress*

timba, *bucket, pail; dipper*
tinggal, *to stay, to remain*
   (33)
tinggi, *high, tall*
tingkat, *storey*
tingkap, *window*
tokong, (Chinese) *temple*
tolong, *to help*
tongkat, *walking-stick*
topi, *hat* (general term)
tua, *old* (of people) (123);
   dark (of colours)
tuala, *towel*

tuan, *lord, master; boss;*
   sir, Mr (101)
tuang, *to pour out; to make*
   (tea) (113)
tuang téh, *to make tea*
tujuh, *seven*
tujuh belas, *seventeen*
tujuh puluh, *seventy*
tukang kebun, *gardener*
tulis, *to write*
turun, *to go down; to come*
   down, to descend; to set
   (of the sun)

U

ubi, *potato*
ubi kayu, *tapioca*
ubi kentang, *potato*
udang, *prawn*
ulangkaji, *revision*
ular, *snake*

ular selimpat, *sea-snake*
untuk, *for; in order to*
urat, *strand;* cl. *for thread*
utas, *skein, string;* cl. *for*
   things in strings; cf.
   Appendix A

W

wah!, *oh dear!*
wak-wak, *gibbon*
warna, *colour*

wayang, *theatrical performance*
wayang gambar, *cinema*

Y

yang, *who, whom, which,*
   that (156–159)
Yang Dipertuan Agung,
   Paramount Ruler
   (the King of Malaysia)

Yang Dipertuan Besar, *the*
   Ruler of Negri Sembilan
Yang Maha Mulia, *His*
   Highness
yang pertama, *first* (93a)

Z

zaman, *time*

APPENDIX G

ENGLISH-MALAY VOCABULARY

See the remarks at the beginning of Appendix F; they apply here also.

a, an, se, satu, q.v.
able, to be, boléh
about (concerning), pasal
according to, ikut
acute, teruk
addition, in, dan lagi
aeroplane, kapalterbang
affected by, to be, kena (120)
afford, to be able to, tahan
  belanja
afraid, to be, takut
after, lepas
after that, lepas itu
afterwards, lepas itu
again, sekali lagi
aged, to be, berumur
ago, dahulu, dulu
agree, bersetuju
alive, to be, hidup (33)
all, semua (144)
all gone, sudah habis
allow, bagi (143)
all right, baiklah
alone, seorang
along (with), sama
a lot (of), banyak (25)
also, dan lagi (150)

always, selalu
among, antara (133)
and, dan
angry, marah; sakit hati (106)
animal, binatang
another time, lain kali
answer (vb.), menjawab
ant, semut
anxious, susah hati (106)
any (adj.), mana-mana (128)
anybody, siapa-siapa (128)
anyone, siapa-siapa (128)
anything, apa-apa (128)
approximately, lebih kurang
arduous, teruk
areca nut, buah pinang
arm, tangan; lengan
arrive, sampai, tiba
as, macam
ascend, naik (40)
as if, macam
ask (inquire), bertanya
ask (invite), jemput
ask for, minta
at, di (14); pada (77)
at first, mula-mula
attap, kajang

B

back, belakang (132)
ball, bola
banana, buah pisang
bandit, pengganas, penjahat
bashful, segan
bathe (wash), mandi
bathroom, bilik air, bilik mandi
bay, teluk
bazaar, pasar
be, ada (22)
be able, boléh
beach, pantai
be alive, hidup
bean, kacang
beat (vb.), pukul
beautiful, bagus; cantik
   (pretty)
be burned down, terbakar
because, keṛana, sebab
become, jadi
bed, tempat tidur (general
   term); katil (European
   style); pangking (sleeping platform as found in
   servants' quarters)
bedroom, bilik; bilik tidur
bee, lebah
beef, daging lembu
beetle, kumbang
before (formerly), dahulu,
   dulu
before (place), depan (132)
before (time), sebelum
begin, mula, mulai (96)
behind, belakang (132)
below, bawah (132)
belt, talipinggang
be married, berkahwin
beneath, bawah (132)

bersanding, bersanding (109)
best quality, nombor satu
beside, sebelah (133)
betel nut, buah pinang
better, had, baik (39)
between, antara (133)
beyond, lepas
bicycle, basikal
big, besar
bird, burung
bit, a, sikit
bitter, pahit
black, hitam
blanket, selimut
blouse, baju
blue, biru
body, badan
boil (vb.) rebus
book, buku
bookshop, kedai buku
born, to be, dilahirkan
borrow, to, pinjam (142)
boss, tuan
box (big), kotak besar
box (small), kotak
boy, budak; budak laki-laki
brassière, baju dalam péndék
bread, roti
breakfast (vb. and n.). makan
   pagi
bridal throne, pelamin
bride, pengantin; pengantin
   perempuan
bridegroom, pengantin;
   pengantin laki-laki
bring, bawa
broad (of shoulders), bidang,
   cf. Appendix A

broadcast (n.), siaran
broken, patah
brown, pérang
bucket, timba
bud, kuntum, pucuk, cf.
   Appendix A
buffalo, kerbau
building, bangunan
bullock-cart, keréta lembu

burned down, to be, terbakar
bus, bas;
but, tetapi, tapi
butcher's shop, kedai daging
butt-end, puntung, cf. Appendix
   A
butter, mentéga
buy, beli
by oneself, seorang

C

cabbage, kobis
cadjan, kajang
café, kedai kopi
call (vb.), panggil
call at, singgah
call in, singgah
can (vb.), boléh
candle, lilin
car, keréta
carry, bawa
cart, keréta
casting-net, jala
cat, kucing
catch (vb.), tangkap
catch fire, terbakar
catty, kati
cause, sebab
cent, sén
   ten cents, sepuluh sén
    (S. Malaya)
   ten cents, sekupang
    (N. Malaya)
centipede, lipan
ceremony, istiadat
certain, tentu
certainly, tentu
chair, kerusi
cheap, murah

cheese, kéju
chest, dada
chick (window-blind),
   bidai
chicken, ayam
child (offspring), anak
child (youngster), budak
chillies, cabai
China, Negeri China
Chinese (adj.), Cina
Chinese (person), orang Cina
Chinese (language), bahasa
   Cina
church, geréja
cicada, riang-riang
cigar, rokok
cigarette, rokok
cinema, panggung wayang
   (gambar)
civet-cat, musang
clean (vb.), cuci
clever, pandai
clock, jam
cloth, kain
clothes, pakaian
clothing, pakaian
cloud, awan
coat, baju

cockroach, lipas
coconut, nyiur
coffee, kopi
coffee-shop, kedai kopi
cold, sejuk
colour, warna
come, datang, mari (41)
come back, balik
come down, turun
come in, masuk
come out, keluar
come too, datang sama,
     mari sama (69)
come up, naik
command (vb.), suruh
completed, sudah (11)–111)
composition (essay), karangan
compound (of a house),
     kampung

concerning, pasal
confluence, kuala
cook (n.), kuki
cook (vb.), masak
cord, tali
cost, belanja; harganya (56)
count (vb.), bilang
country, negeri
cow, lembu; lembu betina
crab, ketam
crate, tong
crockery, pinggan mangkuk
crow (n.) burung gagak
cup, cawan
cupboard, almari, lemari
curry, gulai
curve (n.), bentuk, cf.
     Appendix A
cut off, potong

D

dangerous, berbahaya
dark, gelap
dark (of colours), tua
daughter, anak; anak
     perempuan
day, hari
day after tomorrow, the,
     lusa
day before yesterday, the,
     kelmarin dahulu
dead (adj.), mati
dead, to be, mati
dear (expensive), mahal
debt, hutang
debt, to be in, berhutang
demand (vb.), minta
descend, turun
dew, embun

die, mati
different, lain
difficult, susah
diligent, rajin
dining-room, bilik makan
dipper, timba
dirty, kotor
dish, pinggan
ditch, parit
do, buat
doctor, doktor
dog, anjing
dollar, ringgit
don't, jangan (146)
don't ever, jangan sekali-
     kali (149)
door, pintu
drain, parit

dress (woman's frock), gaun
drink (vb.), minum
drive a car, bawa kereta
dry, kering
duck, itik

durian, buah durian
dutiable, to be, kena cukai
duty (customs), cukai
dwell, duduk (33)

E

each, tiap-tiap
ear, telinga
earlier (formerly), dahulu, dulu
earth, tanah
easy, senang
eat, makan
edge, tepi
education, pelajaran
egg, telur
eight, lapan, delapan (49)
eighteen, lapan belas;
  delapan belas (49)
eighty, lapan puluh; delapan
  puluh (49)
electric, elektrik
elephant, gajah
eleven, sebelas
else, lagi
employee, pekerja
empty, kosong
end (finish), akhir
endure, tahan
English (adj.), Inggeris
English (language), bahasa
  Inggeris; bahasa orang
  putih (31)

English (people), *the*, orang
  Inggeris
enough, cukup
essay, karangan
estuary, kuala
etc., d.s.b.
etcetera, dan sebagainya
European (adj.; n.), orang putih
even, pun (130)
evening, malam; petang (97)
  (124)
every, tiap-tiap
every evening, tiap-tiap malam;
every month, tiap-tiap bulan;
every night, tiap-tiap malam;
every year, tiap-tiap tahun;
examination, peperiksaan
excellent, bagus
excess, in, lebih
excuse (vb.), maafkan
exist, ada (22)
expense, belanja
expensive, mahal
eye, mata

F

face, muka
fall down, terjatuh
fall downstairs, terjatuh
　tangga
fast, cepat
fat, gemuk
father, bapa
fear (vb.), takut
feast, kenduri
federal, persekutuan
federation, persekutuan
Federation of Malaya,
　Persekutuan Tanah
　Melayu
fellow!, poor, kasihan dia!
female, perempuan, betina
　(13)
feminine, perempuan,
　betina (13)
fence, pagar
fetch, ambil
fever, demam
fever, to have a, demam
fifteen, lima belas
fifty, lima puluh
film (in the cinema), gambar
fine (good), bagus
fine (n.), denda
fined, to be, kena denda
finger, jari
finish, habis
finished, sudah (110–111);
　habis
fire, api
fire, to catch, terbakar
firefly, kelip-kelip
first (adj.), yang pertama (93a)
first (adv.), dahulu, dulu
first, at, mula-mula

first-class, nombor satu
fish, ikan
fish-hook, kail
fit (well, healthy), sihat
five, lima
flesh, daging
floods, air bah
floor, lantai
flour, tepung
flower, bunga
fly (n.), lalat
fly (vb.), terbang
follow, ikut
food, makanan
foot, kaki
football, bolasépak
foreign, asing
forest, hutan, rimba
forget, terlupa
forgive, maafkan
fork, garfu
forty, empat puluh
four, empat
fourteen, empat belas
fractured, patah
French beans, kacang buncis
Friday, hari Jumaat
friend, kawan
frightened, takut
from, dari; daripada (35a) (92)
from there, dari sana
from where, dari mana
front, depan (132)
fruit, buah; buahan (61)
fruit-market, pasar buah-
　buahan
fry, goréng
frying-pan, kuali
furthermore, dan lagi

G

garden, kebun
gardener, tukang kebun
gecko, cicak
general (adj.), agung
geography, ilmu bumi
Georgetown, Tanjung (82)
get (fetch), ambil
get (obtain), dapat
get married, berkahwin
get up, bangun
gibŁɔn, wak-wak
girl, budak; budak perem-
   puan
gloves, sarungtangan
go, pergi
   go at once, pergi lekas
   go back, balik
   go down, turun
   go in, masuk
   go on foot, berjalan kaki
   go shopping, pergi beli
      barang

go to bed, tidur
go to sleep, tidur
go up, naik
goat, kambing
going to, to be, hendak,
   nak (62)
golf ball, bola golf
good, baik
good (of food), sedap
good at, pandai
goods, barang
goose, angsa
gone, all, sudah habis
government, kerajaan
grain, a, butir, cf.
   Appendix A
grass, rumput
great, besar
green, hijau
grey, kelabu
guilty, salah
gun, senapang

H

had better, baik (39)
hair, rambut
half, setengah
hand, tangan
handkerchief, saputangan
hang, to, gantung
hang about, lengah
hanged, to be, kena gantung
hard (of work), kuat
hardworking, rajin
hat (general term), topi
hat (Malay style), songkok

have, ada (22)
have a bath, mandi
have a holiday, bercuti
have breakfast, makan pagi
he, dia
head, kepala
headland, tanjung
headmaster, guru besar
headmistress, guru besar
healthy, sihat
hear, dengar
heart, jantung; hati (106)

he himself, dia sendiri
help (vb.), tolong
her (obj.), dia
her (possessive), dia; nya
  (17)
here, di sini
here (hither), ke sini
hide (intrans.), bersembunyi
high, tinggi
Highness, His, Yang
  Maha Mulia
hill, bukit
him, dia
Hindu (adj.), Hindu
Hindu (n.), orang Hindu
hire, séwa
hire-car, keréta séwa
his, dia; nya (17)
His Highness, Yang
  Maha Mulia

hither, ke sini
hold out (endure), tahan.
hole, lobang
hornet, tebuan
horse, kuda
hot (general term), hangat
  (70)
hot (of pepper, etc.),
  pedas (70)
hot (of the sun), panas (70)
how, macam mana
how long, berapa lama
how many, berapa
how much, berapa
hundred, ratus
  a hundred, seratus
  one hundred, seratus
hurry (to leave quickly),
  pergi lekas
hurt (of feelings), kěcil hati

I

I, saya
idle (vb.), léngah
if, kalau
in, di, (14); dalam (132)
indebted, berhutang
independence, kemerdékaan
independent, merdéka
India, Negeri India
Indian (adj.), India
Indian (n.),orang India

inform, kata kepada
ink, dakwat
inquire, bertanya
insect, serangga
inside, dalam (132)
intend to, hendak, nak (62)
invite, jemput
island, pulau
issued, to be (of books), terbit

J

jacket, baju
Japanese (adj.), Jepun
Japanese (n.), orang Jepun
Japanese (language), bahasa
  Jepun
jewel, permata

Johore, Negeri Johor
Johore Bahru, Johor Baharu
jump lompat
jungle, hutan, rimba
just now, tadi

K

Kedah, Negeri Kedah
keep (store), simpan
Kelantan, Negeri Kelantan
kettle, cérék
kick, sépak

kind (sort), macam
kitchen, dapur
know (a fact), tahu
know how to, tahu
Kota Bharu, Kota Baharu

L

ladder, tangga
lady's fingers, kacang bendi
land, tanah
language, bahasa
large, besar
last (vb.), tahan
last (preceding), lepas
last month, bulan lepas
last night, semalam
last week, minggu lepas
last year, tahun lepas
late, lambat, léwat (100)
lazy, malas
lead (vb.), bawa
leaf, daun
learn, belajar
leave (vb.), bertolak
leave, to be on, bercuti
leave, to go on, bercuti
leg, kaki
lend, pinjamkan, bagi
  pinjam (142–143)
lesson, pelajaran
let (allow), bagi (143)
letter, surat
light (of colours), muda
lightning, kilat

like (vb.), suka
like (prep.), macam
like that, macam itu
like this, macam ini
lion, singa
listen, dengar
listen to, dengar
little, kecil
little, a, sikit
live (be alive), hidup (33)
live (dwell), duduk (33)
liver, hati (106)
loaf of bread, a, sebantal
  roti
look, téngok
look at, téngok
look for, cari
long, panjang
long (of time), lama
lord, tuan
lot (of), *a*, banyak (25)
lottery, loteri
low, rendah
lucky, mujur
  that's lucky!, mujurlah!
luggage, barang
lump (piece), keping

M

maidservant, amah

make, buat

make (cause to), bagi (143)

make coffee, bancuh kopi, buat kopi (113)

make tea, tuang téh, buat téh (113)

Malacca (state), Negeri Melaka

Malacca (town), Melaka

Malay (adj), Melayu

Malay (language), bahasa Melayu

Malay (person), orang Melayu

Malaya, Malaya; Tanah Melayu

male, laki-laki, jantan (13)

man, orang; orang laki-laki

manage to, dapat

mangosteen, buah manggis

mantis, cencada

many, banyak, ramai (25)

market, pasar

married (adj.), berkahwin

masculine, laki-laki, jantan (13)

mason-bee, angkut-angkut

master, tuan

matter, it doesn't, tak apa (71)

mattress, tilam

me, saya

meat, daging

mention it, don't, sama-sama (79)

middle, tengah (133)

milk, susu

million, juta

  a million, sejuta

  one million, sejuta

minute (60 seconds), minit

mist, kabut

mix, bancuh

moment, a, sekejap

Monday, hari Senin

money, duit

monkey, kera

month, bulan

moon, bulan

more, lagi

  the more ... the more, lagi ... lagi

more (in excess), lebih

more (in excess), lebih

more or less, lebih kurang

morning, pagi

morning, this; pagi ini

morning, this (past only), pagi tadi

mosque; mesjid

mosquito, nyamuk

mosquito-net, kelambu

mother, emak

motive, sebab

mount (vb.), naik (40)

mountain, gunung

mouse, tikus

mousedeer, pelanduk

mouth, mulut

move (house), berpindah

move (trans.), alih

move off, bertolak

Mr, Encik; Tuan

much, banyak (25)

museum, muzium

mutton, daging kambing

my, saya (17) (20)

N

nail (finger, toe, etc.), kuku
name, nama
national, kebangsaan
National Language, Bahasa
  Kebangsaan
neck, léhér
needle, jarum
need to, *no*, tak payah
  (147c)
Negri Sembilan, Negeri
  Sembilan
new, baharu
news, khabar
newspaper, suratkhabar
next (following), depan
next-door to, sebelah (133)
next month, bulan depan
next time, lain kali
next to, sebelah (133)
next week, minggu depan
next year, tahun depan

night, malam
nightdress, baju tidur
nine, sembilan
nineteen, sembilan belas
ninety, sembilan puluh
no, bukan (2); tidak (7);
  belum (110–111); dak,
  tak
no need to, tak payah (147c)
nose, hidung
not, bukan (2); tidak (7);
  belum (110–111); dak,
  tak
not at all, sama-sama (79)
not very, tak berapa
not yet, belum, tidak lagi
  (110–111)
nought, kosong
now, sekarang
number, nombor

O

obtain, dapat
o'clock, pukul (94)
off, dari atas (132)
office, pejabat
offspring, anak
off to, *to be*, hendak
  ke, nak ke (64)
oh dear!, wah!
O.K., baiklah
old (of people), tua
old (of things), lama
old, *to be* (so many (years)),
  berumur
on, pada (77); di atas (132)

once, sekali
one, satu, se- (44)
onion, bawang
only, sahaja
on to, ke atas (132)
open (adj.), terbuka
open (vb.), buka
orange, buah limau
order (vb.), suruh
originally, mula-mula
our, kita (17)
outside, di luar
over (finished), sudah habis
ox, lembu

P

Pahang, Negeri Pahang
palm-frond, kajang
panties (women's), seluar dalam
paper, kertas
Paramount Ruler, Yang Dipertuan Agung
part, bahagian
party (social), kenduri
pass (examinations), lulus dalam (peperiksaan)
passenger, penumpang
patient (n.), orang sakit
pay (n.), gaji
pay (vb.), bayar
peace, selamat (26)
peas, kacang hijau
pen, kalam
Penang (island), Pulau Pinang, Tanjung (82)
Penang (state), Negeri Pinang
peninsula, semenanjung
pension, pencen
people, orang
pepper, lada putih
Perak, Negeri Pérak
performance, theatrical, wayang
perhaps, barangkali
Perlis, Negeri Perlis
person, orang
picture, gambar
piece, keping
pig, babi
pillow, bantal
pity (n.), kasihan

place (n.), tempat
plate, pinggan
play (vb.), bermain
pleased, suka hati
pocket, pokét
point (headland), tanjung
policeman, mata-mata
poor (not rich), miskin
poor fellow!, kasihan dia!
pork, daging babi
Portuguese (adj.), Portugis
Portuguese (people), orang Portugis
Post Office, Pejabat Pos
potato, ubi; ubi kentang
pour out, tuang (113)
pour out tea, bancuh téh (113)
prawn, udang
pray, sembahyang
prayer, sembahyang
prefer, lagi suka
pretty, cantik
previously, dahulu, dulu
price, harga
primary (education), rendah
primary school, sekolah rendah
prince, raja
programme (radio), siaran
proud (in a good sense), besar hati (106)
Province Wellesley, Seberang Perai
put, bubuh
put away, simpan
put on (clothes), pakai
pyjamas, baju tidur

Q

quality, *best*, nombor satu
quarter, suku

quick, cepat
quickly, cepat

R

rain, hujan
rajah, raja
rambutan, buah rambutan
rat, tikus
rather, sikit (83)
raw, mentah
razor, pisau cukur
reach, sampai
read, baca
ready, siap
real, sungguh
really, sungguh
receive, terima, dapat
red, mérah
remain, tinggal
remember, ingat
restaurant, kedai makan
return, balik
revision, ulangkaji
rice (cooked), nasi
rice (growing), padi
rice (uncooked), beras
rice-field, bendang, sawah

rich, kaya
rickshaw, béca
ride (in, on), naik (40)
ring (n.), cincin
ripe, masak
rise (get up), bangun
rise (sun), terbit
river, sungai
road, jalan
roast (vb.), panggang
roll (of cloth), kayu, cf.
    Appendix A
roof, bumbung
room, bilik
rope, tali
rubber, getah
rubber estate, kebun getah
rubber-tapper, penoréh getah
rubber-tree, pokok getah
Ruler (of Negri Sembilan),
    Yang Dipertuan Besar
run, berlari
run away, lari

S

safe, selamat
safety, selamat (26)
saffron, kunyit
sago, sagu
sail, to set, bertolak

salary, gaji
salt, garam
same, sama
same, the, semacam
same to you, sama-sama

sand, pasir
sarung, kain; kain sarung
Saturday, hari Sabtu
saucer, piring
save money, simpan duit
say, kata, berkata
school, sekolah
scorpion, kala
sea, laut
sea-snake, ular selimpat
second (1/60 of a minute), saat
secondary (education), menengah
secondary school, sekolah menengah
see, nampak; téngok (42)
seed, biji
seek, cari
Selangor, Negeri Selangor
self, sendiri
sell, jual
separate (adj.), asing
seriously ill, sakit teruk
set (of the sun), turun
set sail, bertolak
seven, tujuh
seventeen, tujuh belas
seventy, tujuh puluh
severe (serious), teruk
shall, hendak, nak (62)
shave (intrans.), bercukur
shave (trans.), cukur
she, dia
sheath, sarung
sheet, selimut
ship, kapal
shirt, baju keméja
shoes, kasut
shoot (n.), pucuk, cf. Appendix A
shoot (vb.), tembak
shop, kedai

shopkeeper, orang kedai
shopping, to do some, beli barang
shore, pantai
short, péndék
shorts, seluar péndék
side, tepi (133)
sir, tuan
sit, duduk
sit in state side by side, bersanding (109)
six, enam
sixteen, enam belas
sixty, enam.puluh
skein, utas, cf. Appendix A
sleep, tidur
sleeve, tangan
slice, potong, cf. Appendix A
slip (woman's), baju dalam panjang
slow, lambat
slowly, lambat-lambat
small, kecil
smoke (vb.), hisap
snake, ular
snake, sea-, ular selimpat
soap, sabun
socks, sarungkaki péndék
soon, sekejap lagi
son, anak, anak laki-laki
sort (kind), macam
sour, masam
soya beans, kacang soya
soya sauce, tauyu
speak, bercakap
splendid, bagus
spoon, camca
staircase, tangga
stairs, tangga
stalk, tangkai, cf. Appendix A
stand (vb.), berdiri
stand (endure), tahan

stand up, berdiri
start (vb.), bertolak
state (n.), negeri
station, stesen
stay (behind), tinggal (33)
stay (in a hotel, etc.),
   duduk (33)
steamship, kapal api
stem, tangkai, cf. Appendix A
still (adv.), lagi
stockings, sarungkaki
   panjang
stomach, perut
stop (vb.), berhenti
stop off, singgah
store (vb.), simpan
storey, tingkat

storm, ribut
strand, urat, cf. Appendix A
strike (vb.), pukul
string, tali; utas, cf.
   Appendix A
strong, kuat
stub, puntung, cf. Appendix A
stupid, bodoh
suddenly, tiba-tiba
sufficient, cukup
sugar, gula
sultan, sultan
sun, matahari
Sunday, hari Ahad
sweet, manis
swim, berenang
sword, pedang

T

table, méja
tail, ékor
take (a thing), ambil
take (a person), bawa
tall, tinggi
Tamil (adj.), Tamil
Tamil (language), bahasa
   Tamil (person), orang
   Tamil
tap (n.), pili
tapioca, ubikayu
tap rubber, *to*, toréh getah
tasteless, tawar
tasty, sedap
tax (n.), cukai
taxable, *to be*, kena cukai
taxi, keréta sewa
tea (dry leaves), daun téh
tea (liquid), téh
teacher, guru
tell (command), suruh

tell (inform), kata kepada
temple (Chinese), tokong
temple (Hindu), kuil
ten, sepuluh
terrorist, pengganas, penjahat
thank you, terima kasih (36)
that, itu
that (rel.), yang (156–159)
that way (direction), ikut itu
that way (thus), macam itu
theatrical performance,
   wayang
the more ... the more ...,
   lagi ... lagi ...
thence, dari sana
there, di sana
there (thither), ke sana
these, ini
thin, kurus
thing, barang
think (opine), ingat

thirteen, tiga belas
thirty, tiga puluh
this, ini
this way (direction), ikut ini
this way (thus), macam ini
thither, ke sana
those, itu
thousand, ribu
  a thousand, seribu
  one thousand, seribu
thread (n.), benang
three, tiga
throne, bridal, pelamin
thumb, ibu jari
thunder, guruh-gemuruh
Thursday, hari Khamis
thus, macam ini, macam itu
tie (n.), taliléhér
tiger, harimau, rimau
time (occasion), kali
time (period), masa, zaman
time to, enough, sempat
time to, no, tak sempat
tin (ore), bijih timah
tin-mine, lombong bijih
  timah
to, ke, kepada (34a)
today, hari ini

toe, jari kaki
toilet (W.C.), jamban
tomorrow, bésok, ésok
tomorrow, the day after
  lusa
too (also), sama; cf. (50)
too late, lewat (100)
tooth, gigi
top, atas (132)
top of, on, di atas (132)
towel, tuala
town, pekan, bandar
train (railway), kerétapi
travel (by, in, on), naik (40)
tree, pokok
Trengganu. Negeri
  Trengganu
trishaw, béca
trousers, seluar panjang
true, sungguh
try, cuba
Tuesday, hari Selasa
turban, serban
turkey, ayam Belanda
twelve, dua belas
twenty, dua puluh
twice, dua kali
two, dua

U

umbrella, payung
under, bawah (132)
underneath, bawah (132)
underpants, seluar dalam
undervest, baju dalam
university, sekolah tinggi

until, sampai
us, kita
use (vb.), pakai
useful, berguna
usually, selalu; biasanya

V

vehicle, keréta
verandah (European), beranda
verandah (Malay), serambi
very, sangat (59); sungguh

very much, sangat (591)
very, not, tak berapa
village, kampung
vinegar, cuka

W

wages, gaji
waist, pinggang
wait, nanti
wait for, nantikan
walk, berjalan, berjalan kaki (141)
walk about, berjalan-jalan
walking-stick, tongkat
wall (outside), témbok
wall (partition), dinding
want, mahu
wardrobe, almari
wash, mandi
wash the clothes, cuci kain
wash up the dishes, cuci pinggan
wasp, penyengat
watch (n.). jam
watch (vb.), téngok
water, air
way, jalan
W.C., jamban
we, kita
wear, pakai
Wednesday, hari Rabu
week, minggu
well (healthy), sihat
wet, basah
what, apa
when, bila; masa (105)
whence, dari mana
where, di mana

where ... from, dari mana
where ... to, ke mana
which, mana
which (rel.) yang (156—159)
while, masa (105)
white, putih
whither, ke mana
who, siapa
who (rel.), yang (156—159)
whom, siapa
whom (rel.), yang (156—159)
why, pasal apa
wicked, jahat
wife, isteri
will (vb.), hendak, nak (62)
win a lottery, menang
window, tingkap
with, dengan
woman, orang; orang perempuan
wood, kayu
word, perkataan
work (n.), kerja
work (vb.), bekerja
work hard, to, bekerja kuat
worker, pekerja
worried, susah hati
write, tulis
writing-paper, kertas tulis
wrong (guilty), salah

Y

year, tahun
yellow, kuning
yesterday, semalam
yesterday, the day before,
   kelmarin dahulu
yet, lagi

yet, not, belum (110–111);
   tidak lagi
you, encik
young, muda
youngster, budak
your, encik (17)

NOTES

TIMES LEARN MALAY

Malay in 3 Weeks *by John Parry and Sahari Sulaiman*
A teach-yourself Malay book that enables you to communicate in practical everyday situations.

Malay Made Easy *by A.W. Hamilton*
How to speak Malay intelligibly and accurately.

Easy Malay Vocabulary: 1001 Essential Words *by A.W. Hamilton*
A handbook to enlarge your vocabulary and to ensure effective communication in Malay on a wide range of topics.

Speak Malay! *by Edward S. King*
A graded course in simple spoken Malay for English-speaking people.

Write Malay *by Edward S. King*
A more advanced course on how to read and write good modern Malay.

Learn Malay: A Phrase a Day *by Dr. G. Soosai*
A simple but comprehensive way to learn Malay in 365 days.

Converse in Malay *by Dr. G. Soosai*
A compilation of the highly successful RTM *Radio Lessons* series, a programme which proved both popular and beneficial to thousands of listeners in mastering Malay.

Malay Phrase Book For Tourists *by Hj Ismail Ahmad & Andrew Leonki*
The indispensable companion, it helps tourists in everyday situations in a Malay-speaking world.

Standard Malay Made Simple *by Dr. Liaw Yock Fang*
An intensive Standard Malay language (bahasa Melayu baku) course designed for adult learners with no previous knowledge of the Malay language.

Speak Standard Malay: A Beginner's Guide *by Dr. Liaw Yock Fang*
An easy and comprehensive guide which enables you to acquire fluency and confidence in speaking standard Malay in only 3 months.

TIMES LEARN INDONESIAN

Standard Indonesian Made Simple *by Dr. Liaw Yock Fang with Dra Nini Tiley-Notodisuryo*
An intensive Standard Indonesian language course designed for beginners to gain mastery of the language.

Speak Standard Indonesian: A Beginner's Guide *by Dr. Liaw Yock Fang with Drs. Munadi Patmadiwiria & Abdullah Hassan*
An easy and comprehensive guide which enables you to acquire fluency and confidence in speaking Indonesian in only a few months.

Indonesian In 3 Weeks *by Dr. Liaw Yock Fang with Drs. Munadi Patmadiwiria*
A teach-yourself Indonesian book that enables you to understand what people say to you, and to make yourself understood in everyday situations.

Easy Indonesian Vocabulary: 1001 Essential Words *by Dr. Liaw Yock Fang*
A handbook to enlarge your vocabulary and to ensure effective communication in Indonesian on a wide range of topics.

Indonesian Phrase Book For Tourists *by Nini Tiley-Notodisuryo*
A handy reference for every traveller, it helps you in everyday situations during your stay in Indonesia.

DICTIONARY/THESAURUS

Times Comparative Dictionary of Malay-Indonesian Synonyms
compiled by Dr. Leo Suryadinata, edited by Professor Abdullah Hassan
For learners of Malay and Indonesian who want to know the differences that exist between the two languages.

Tesaurus Bahasa Melayu *by Prof. Madya Noor Ein Mohd Noor, Noor Zaini Mohd Ali, Mohd Tahir Abd Rahman, Singgih W. Sumartoyo, Siti Fatimah Ariffin*
A comprehensive A–Z thesaurus that enables you to master Malay vocabulary effectively.